"Jack draws a straight line f̶͟͞r̶͟͞o̶͟͞m̶ ... t̶e̶a̶c̶h̶i̶n̶g̶ and under representation of biblical mercy *in* the church to the lack of love so many feel *from* the church. From the familiar Samaritan parable, he unpacks God's pattern of love of see, go, do, and endure and gives a practical and helpful diagnostic. He reminds us that true healing, justice, and reconciliation begin with the impulse of mercy toward our neighbors and enemies. I heartily recommend this book."

Dr. Timothy Keller, pastor emeritus and founder, Redeemer Presbyterian Church; chairman, Redeemer City to City

"Jack reminds us that while God is often portrayed in culture as a harsh and distant master, he is in fact a loving father who longs to grow closer to us—and for us to show mercy to one another."

Andy Stanley, author, communicator, and founder of North Point Ministries

"This book is worth reading! It's a revolutionary lens on life, the character of God, spiritual formation, and the church that will provoke the kind of deep reflection and evaluation that always precedes significant life change. It is by far the most insightful study and application of mercy I've ever read. I highly recommend it."

Chip Ingram, teaching pastor, Living on the Edge; author of *The Real God: How He Longs for You to See Him*

"*The God Impulse* takes us on a journey through the rich, wonderful, transforming power of mercy. Throughout the book, Jack reminds us that mercy is more than a sentiment or feeling. It is tied to truth and is a picture of the heart and nature of our great God. I love the way Jack describes the relationship between mercy and truth: 'mercy and truth are the core of "religious" ligaments that reconnect us.' As you read this wonderful book you will find yourself celebrating the beauty and power of mercy."

Dr. Crawford W. Loritts Jr., author, speaker, radio host, and senior pastor of Fellowship Bible Church

"In *The God impulse,* Jack Alexander reminds us, and indeed challenges us, to understand the vital importance of mercy. Mercy moved God to save us—and mercy sustains us. Anyone who claims to be 'a follower of Jesus' is compelled to be an imitator of Jesus. I have been blessed and challenged by *The God Impulse*, and I know you will too."

Michael Youssef, president of Leading The Way Ministries

"*The God Impulse* is both a refreshing breeze and a slap in the face. Jack Alexander makes the case that mercy is one of the defining characteristics of God and as such should be the same for those who follow him. Honestly, I was aggravated and convicted at times, but more so, I was encouraged and motivated to remember who Jesus calls us to be as Christians. I love a book that can convict and inspire me simultaneously. This one did. Oh, and the way the author unpacks the story of the Good Samaritan is enough to warrant a second reading."

Clayton King, president, Crossroads Summer Camps and Missions; teaching pastor, Newspring Church; author of *Stronger* and *Overcome*

"A rare and exceptional book on mercy—by a rare and exceptional man of mercy. Do yourself and others a favor by reading this book. And when you do, get ready to fall in love with the beauty of mercy."

Randy Pope, pastor, Perimeter Church

"Powerful. Deep. *The God Impulse* is the best book I have ever read on the mercy attribute of God and its implications for living a godly life. Thank you, Jack, for your insights and for the incredible work you have invested. A true kingdom treasure."

Robert Lupton, founder and president, FCS Urban Ministries; author of *Toxic Charity* and *Charity Detox*

"Jesus describes compassion and mercy in the language of the visceral. He intended for mercy and compassion to be something that we feel, not a subject we discuss. Sadly, too many Christians never see the circumstances that trap people's souls long enough to 'feel' anything. We choose to ignore it or finance the heroic work done by others when Jesus actually calls us to be the people of mercy ourselves. In *The God Impulse*, Jack Alexander causes us to feel again, to be both inspired and encouraged to action."

Dr. Charlie Dates, senior pastor, Progressive Baptist Church; affiliate professor, Trinity Evangelical Divinity School

"There are so many things we want for ourselves that we do not offer to others. We want love, but we don't return it. We want money, but we don't give it. Deep down in our souls, knowing our sinful nature, we want mercy more than anything else. Yet we struggle to offer mercy to others. But as *The God Impulse* makes imminently clear, God's merciful acts toward us convey his compelling request for us to show mercy to others. If only we would answer his call."

"The idea of this book might be the most attractive shape of my faith I could ever aspire to live. If more of us could live out the type of mercy discussed in *The God Impulse*, it would change the view of the Christian faith everywhere."

"*Mercy* is a word we can use today, particularly in the context of the current climate of our country and world. Jack introduces or reintroduces us to the concept of mercy. Not just the knowledge of it but the radical practice of it. It is important to be reminded of mercy's role in saving us and in how we share it with our neighbor. Hopefully, this work will stir many to go from recipients of mercy to distributors of mercy, especially among those who might not look like us."

"My gauge for a high-praise book is the number of turned-down pages to which I will return to do hard and beautiful work in my life. This one has sixty-seven, far above average. *The God Impulse* will help me, and many others in multiple cultures, offer fresh and powerful mercy."

"*Mercy* has become a popular word within our cultural and political climate. While some attempt to embrace it with great eagerness, and others avoid it with blithe indifference, many have missed the holistic nature of mercy. . . . Jack is careful not to divorce justice from mercy, which would render mercy as mere sentimentality. In the same manner, he does not divorce mercy from justice, which would render justice as harsh and severe. *The God Impulse* is a clarion call to truly embody the heart of God while reminding us that mercy is his heartbeat."

"This book is an exposition of one of the most celebrated stories in the Bible—perhaps in all of literature—the parable of the Good

Samaritan. The author holds high the parable as a model for radical and merciful Christian engagement. This timeless and timely exhortation reminds us that it is within this context of relationships that the tension between truth and mercy is best reconciled."

David Allman, chairman, Regent Partners

"*The God Impulse* provides a pattern for loving others the way God has loved us through Christ Jesus. Jack Alexander uses the parable of the Good Samaritan to educate, inspire, and challenge us to see, go, do, and endure, just as Christ does for each of us."

Lee B. Torrence, cofounder of Regenerated Communities

"Take out your highlighter, because you're going to use it! Then get ready to become a living example of God's mercy to your friends, neighbors, and total strangers. *The God Impulse* unpacks the meaning of true mercy as Jesus taught and ultimately modeled it. In these pages, Jack provides a master class that is inspiring, simple, and very practical—and that every one of us needs."

Shaunti Feldhahn, social researcher, speaker, bestselling author of *For Women Only*, *For Men Only*, and *The Kindness Challenge*

"The genius of this book is its unanticipated subtlety. Jack Alexander refuses to stop with an obvious plea for Christian engagement with the world's needs. He makes that case, to be sure, but his greater urgency is for the needs of those who have. To refuse to become involved does not merely deprive those who have liabilities; in a way potentially more tragic, non-involvement robs those with assets of their authentic identity and assigned vocation. This book is a gentle warning and an earnest plea. As such, it can hardly be bettered."

Ronnie Stevens, missionary and pastor

"Jack and I first met more than 20 years ago at a CEO gathering in Chicago. I knew he was an outstanding business leader, but immediately sensed something more. What explained his tenderness, his warmth, his unusual attentiveness and genuine interest in others? Reading *The God Impulse* provides the answer. A theme runs deep in Jack's veins. It is the power of applied mercy in the life of a Christian. Jack unpacks this attribute of God's own character in the most extraordinary way. Through this book we realize that we, too, can be instruments of God to others, extending the mercy he has granted us."

John D. Beckett, chairman, The Beckett Companies; author of *Loving Monday* and *Mastering Monday*

The GOD IMPULSE

THE POWER OF MERCY IN AN UNMERCIFUL WORLD

JACK ALEXANDER

BakerBooks
a division of Baker Publishing Group
Grand Rapids, Michigan

Published by Baker Books
a division of Baker Publishing Group
PO Box 6287, Grand Rapids, MI 49516-6287
www.bakerbooks.com

Printed in the United States of America

Library of Congress Cataloging-in-Publication Data
Names: Alexander, Jack, 1951– author.
Title: The God impulse : the power of mercy in an unmerciful world / Jack Alexander.
Description: Grand Rapids : Baker Publishing Group, 2018.
Identifiers: LCCN 2018007046 | ISBN 9780801075292 (pbk.)
Subjects: LCSH: Mercy. | Good Samaritan (Parable)
Classification: LCC BV4647.M4 A44 2018 | DDC 241/.4—dc23
LC record available at https://lccn.loc.gov/2018007046

ISBN 9780801094118 (cloth)

The author is represented by Alive Literary Agency, 7680 Goddard Street, Suite 200, Colorado Springs, CO 80920, www.aliveliterary.com.

18 19 20 21 22 23 · 24   7 6 5 4 3 2

To my three wonderful sons,
John, Kurt, and Matt—
may the world see the mercy and love of God
through your lives. I am so proud of you.

Contents

Foreword by Walter Brueggemann   11

Acknowledgments   15

Introduction: *Do We Bring Hope and Healing?*   17

1. The God Impulse   27

Part 1 SEE: *The Disposition of Mercy*

2. Eight Seconds to See   49

3. The Womb: *Feeling Mercy for the Poor and Distressed*   73

Part 2 GO: *The Discovery of Mercy*

4. The Last Hour   103

5. A Price Paid: *Thinking Mercy for Fellow Sinners*   125

Part 3   DO: *The Displacement of Mercy*

  6. In the Game   153
  7. Hallelujah: *Divine Mercy for Our Enemies*   173

Part 4   ENDURE: *The Discipline of Mercy*

  8. The Two Deals   197
  9. The Covenant of Intimacy   217

      Conclusion: *GASP!*   237
      Notes   241

Foreword

*H*ere is a riddle Jack Alexander might offer us: What has an attention span shorter than a goldfish (nine seconds) and is as dumb as a sheep? Answer: A human person shaped by the rat race of anxiety and greed that dominate our society.

The God Impulse is addressed precisely to company that surely includes most of us, conservatives and liberals. The "way of the world" is to be fearful, self-protective, worried about having enough, and eager to add a nanosecond of well-being to our lives by hustle. To this multitudinous company, Alexander proposes an alternative life rooted in God's own life and expressed and lived out in the daily concreteness of mercy. He draws a straight line from God's own impulse to human acts of mercy that do indeed transform the world.

The plotline of Alexander's exposition is found in the Good Samaritan text that is seen to offer a four-part pattern of love. The odd Samaritan character in the tale, so alien in Jewish culture, is a man who was able to *see* someone in need, willing to *go* to that person, capable of *generous care*, and committed to *enduring long-term care* for them. It traces out the deepest inclination of the gospel: the God who regularly *sees* people in need, gladly *goes* to them, willingly *acts* for them, and faithfully *stays* with them. This book teems with biblical texts in which God performs and re-performs this pattern of love. Alexander is deeply and knowingly grounded in Scripture; his reading of the Bible makes a pivotal accent on God's mercy inescapable. This is God's deepest impulse. It is what God most wants to do and most readily does.

But Alexander has not written the book primarily as a witness to God's mercy, even though his attestation to the God of mercy is everywhere in the book. Rather the book is a compelling summons and a winsome invitation to us, his readers, to embrace God's impulse as our own.

The book will be of immense interest to conservative Christians who tend, by a reductionist packaging of the gospel, not to see or go to human need because the gospel story is made much too vertical. But the book will be equally of immense interest to liberal Christians. The latter, of which I am one, readily embrace the first step of seeing and pondering human need. It may be what we do best. But where liberal Christians often fail is in a readiness to actually go to human need. Liberal Christians love to talk about and analyze human issues of need. Or they act but do not follow through. Thus, Alexander's third and fourth steps of God's impulse—to do and to endure—matter enormously. The third step—do—requires displacement, being drawn out of one's comfort zone to be fully present to the person in need and on that person's terms. Thus, the Good Samaritan had to stop, perhaps dismount, and turn aside. Such an inconvenience is not easy or normal in a selfie culture. And the fourth step, endurance, or disciplined durability, is difficult because our self-indulgent consumerism is elementally resistant to the discipline of mercy that entails staying with people in need for a long time.

Alexander's book is a powerful account of God's "strange arithmetic" (whereby God blesses those who sometimes are called to go against their own sensibilities toward sinners and enemies) that completely contradicts our society of greed and anxiety. Our usual calculation is with a sharp pencil in the service of our own advantage. But Alexander, by his deep grounding in gospel faith and his own generous practice of neighborliness, has seen "a more excellent way" of being human. His pattern of love is filled out by seemingly endless concrete stories of self-giving with transformative outcomes. Some are reports on other people of faith. But many of them bear the conviction of Alexander's own life. His is a life of support for abandoned widows, generosity toward business partners, and care for children with various challenges.

The world in which we live wants, as much as possible, to reduce everything and everyone to a tradable commodity. The gospel way contradicts that seduction and affirms that the deepest truth and the deepest satisfactions of our lives are in relationships of trust, steadfastness, and generosity. Relatedness makes all the difference. Relatedness recognizes that we cannot simply throw money at human problems. Conversely, Alexander also sees that mercy entails generous expenditures of money on behalf of restorative justice and rehabilitative compassion.

In his previous book, *The God Guarantee*, Alexander affirms the utter fidelity of God, which permits us to escape from the fear of falling short. *The God Impulse* is an advance

13

of that argument. Alexander outlines the urgent imperative that derives from *The God Guarantee* and the spin-off for human discernment, practice, and policy.

Thus, it is utterly important that in Jesus's parable of the Good Samaritan it is reported that the inquiring lawyer "got it"—the neighbor is the one who showed mercy. Good insight! The lawyer understood the parable. But then Jesus concluded with a terse imperative: "Go and do likewise." We can be like the Good Samaritan. Go, and do to those in need. Go, and do to those who are vulnerable. It is all about mercy!

In the process of Jack writing this book, I have gotten to know him and am pleased to count him as a friend. I know him to be a friend who overflows with energy, who has a plentitude of compelling stories, who has a gift for insightful phrase-making, who is permeated with Scripture, and who is passionate in his commitment and wisely discerning in his observation of text and of world. I anticipate that readers will find Alexander contagious in these pages. He has in mind nothing less than an epidemic of mercy that will shatter the old society of scarcity and fear. In the end it is all to the glory of God. But along the way to that glorification of God is neighborly mercy. The parable of the Good Samaritan was a shock and scandal in Jesus's time. It still is, because the truth of God's mercy contradicts what we have come to think of as normal. No wonder the book ends with a startled "gasp," the gasp of a new truth palpably available for our enactment.

Walter Brueggemann
Professor Emeritus,
Columbia Theological Seminary

Acknowledgments

*F*or some time now, I have sensed that something in the evangelical faith was missing. God placed heralds in my path, such as Bob Lupton, Gary Haugen, Tim Keller, Raymond Harris, Darryl Ford, Lee Torrence, Larry Powell, Charles Buffington, Crawford Loritts, David Allman, and Rick Jackson, who showed me a sturdier and "thicker" gospel. This is the "gospel of the kingdom" of which Jesus repeatedly spoke.

A gospel that while uncompromising in lifting up Christ and his Word, life, death, resurrection, and ascension also radically moves horizontally to the love of our neighbors. This love covers the Good Samaritan's disposition of mercy *and* the need to be displaced in our acts of service and commitment. This mercy love is always costly and is the "thunder" that precedes the "lightning" of the grace of God.

Thanks to the Baker team, especially Chad Allen, Mark Rice, and Eileen Hanson, who embraced this message straightaway. Their choice of this book as a feature title strengthened and encouraged our whole team.

Thanks to the strong work and commitment of Patty Wyngaard, as well as the work of Kristin Jackson and my sister, Beth Baumert, who helped in editing the manuscript.

Special thanks to Paul Asay, who came alongside my efforts with his writing skills to help ensure these concepts came to life.

My friend Lisa Jackson of Alive Literary has been invaluable in the process.

Special thanks go to my wife, Lisa, and my family who have stood with me.

Thank you, God our Father, for your magnificent mercy, which accompanies your amazing grace. Your enduring mercy gives us all hope; your steadfast love never fails. Thank you, Jesus, for completing the greatest act of love and mercy for us on the cross. Thank you, Holy Spirit, for your goodness and mercy that will follow us all the days of our lives until we dwell in the house of the Lord forever.

Introduction

*W*e want God!"

The voices of hundreds of thousands of Polish citizens rolled across Warsaw's Victory Square like thunder. "We want God!" they shouted as Pope John Paul II stood and called the people to participate in a special moment in history.

It was June 2, 1979, and Poland was still trapped behind the Iron Curtain. Communist leaders peered from hotel rooms surrounding the square, few understanding that the trajectory of their country, indeed all of Eastern Europe, was about to change forever. The pope—formerly Karol Józef Wojtyła, cardinal of Krakow, Poland—had just been raised to the pontificate the year before, becoming the first non-Italian pope in more than four hundred years. Now the leader of the Roman Catholic Church was speaking in an atheist country, exhorting the people in his homeland to make an unprecedented stand for Christ.

He told the throngs that man was God's greatest work and that Christ redeemed man. Therefore, man cannot be

17

understood without understanding Jesus. "Christ cannot be kept out of the history of man in any part of the globe, at any longitude or latitude . . . The exclusion of Christ from the history of man is an act against man."[1] Even people who don't believe Jesus was the Son of God—even those who actively oppose him—still live under his dominion and in a history shaped by Christianity.

"Today, here in Victory Square, in the capital of Poland, I am asking with all of you, through the great Eucharistic prayer, that Christ will not cease to be for us an open book of life for the future," John Paul said. "For our *Polish* future."[2]

It seemed as though all of Poland joined their voices in one mighty shout, loud enough to deafen communism itself.

"We want God!" they shouted. "We want God!"[3]

Jesus drew the same sort of crowds. Luke 12:1 says "the crowds grew until thousands were milling about and stepping on each other" (NLT). Imagine thousands gathering in those tiny villages around the Sea of Galilee. What was the attraction? According to Matthew 9:35, Jesus was "proclaiming the good news of the kingdom and healing every disease and sickness" (NIV). Jesus also "sent [the twelve disciples] out to proclaim the kingdom of God and to heal the sick" (Luke 9:2 NIV). People were drawn to the *truth* he proclaimed (preaching) and his repeated displays of *mercy* (healing). This combination was the "secret sauce" that you and I can experience today as well.

The Secret Sauce of Mercy and Truth

In Latin, the root word for religion is *ligare*, which means "to connect, bind, or join." So religion is about reconnecting broken, fallen people with their loving Creator God. Just as ligaments (another word that draws its roots from *ligare*) attach bones to one another, religion connects our souls to God. God's plan is that we receive mercy and truth from him and are then able to pass it on to others. This is the beautiful essence of the gospel. We are reconnected to a loving God, and we bring connection and redemption to one another.

Mercy and truth are the core of "religious" ligaments that reconnect us. In Psalm 25:10, God discloses his operating system: "All the paths of the LORD are mercy and truth unto such as keep his covenant and his testimonies" (KJV).

This coupling of mercy and truth occurs throughout Scripture. We receive an array of benefits by reconnecting with God in this way:

- Favor from God and a good name (see Prov. 3:4)
- Atonement for our iniquity (see Prov. 16:6)
- Power and position is preserved (see Prov. 20:28)
- Mercy and truth are inseparable from God's presence (see Ps. 89:14)
- Mercy and truth are the forerunners of righteousness and peace (see Ps. 85:10)
- Jesus characterized himself in this way (see John 14:6)

We see the revelation of both God's heart and character in mercy and truth. As such, when these get out of balance, we cease being the ligaments that properly connect people to God.

What Happened?

But too often today's religion doesn't bring people together as much as it tears them apart.

The world is growing more secular at a dizzying rate. Those who remain in faith often debate politics and dogma with one another. When the Christian polling organization Barna Group asked young Americans what they thought about Christians, those millennials described us as "hypocritical," "judgmental," and "insensitive."[4] In another recent survey, 46 percent of Americans believed that "religion is part of the problem, not the solution."[5]

We even saw in the 2012 and 2016 US elections an underlying desire for care and mercy. Journalist Peggy Noonan reported that in 2012, the Republicans lost the presidential election on the question, "Who cares about people like you?" Then the tables turned in 2016, when Noonan reported, "Tuesday was, in effect, an uprising of the unprotected."[6]

Impersonalized Truth and Outsourced Mercy

When we read about Jesus, we see over and over again how he brought truth and mercy to the people in the context of relationship. He did not write sermons for others to read. He did not communicate through proxy. Jesus had a way of making every touch, word, and glance very personal.

Think about when he asked the Samaritan woman for a drink (see John 4:4–26). Or when the tax collector Zacchaeus clamored up a tree to see Jesus and Jesus promptly invited himself over to the tax man's house (see Luke 19:1–10). Think about how when Jesus rebuked the Pharisees, he did it to their faces (see Matt. 23:13–39). Or how when Jesus healed a leper, he touched the man's snowy skin (see Matt. 8:3). Or when he rubbed mud in a blind man's eyes and made him see again (see John 9:1–12). What could be more personal than touching a leper's skin or a man's eyes?

Jesus spoke truth and showed mercy, and he always did it with a touch. A glance. A smile. He was always *there*. This "secret sauce" of truth and mercy in the context of relationship changed the world. Today, mercy seems to have devolved into deeds, works, and the administration of scanty diaconal funds. In many churches, mercy clearly takes a back seat to truth in ministry focus and resource allocation.

Today on the internet, with just a few clicks, you can receive the "truth" via thousands of sermons and podcasts without so much as seeing or talking to another living person. Many megachurch pastors turn messages into scripted productions that bring in the "seeker." Often they claim intellectual property (IP) rights to their productions. These productions are geared toward mass consumption—to reach the people rather than connect with the person.

Meanwhile, on the mercy front, nonprofit organizations have been one of the fastest growing segments of our economy. There are 1.6 million of them now, and together they represent 9 percent of our economy. Many of these provide crucial, nonduplicable services in the United States and around the world. However, many are overly bureaucratic or hoard money. Sometimes they even do both.

I don't want to discount the work of these nonprofit ministries and organizations. The purpose of this book is not to critique them but rather to suggest that we're ignoring an important and, I'd argue, more effective way of showing mercy: Face-to-face. Hand-to-hand. Life-on-life. When we show mercy and truth in a relational context, the power of the gospel is augmented and multiplied.

The Pattern of Love

This is a book about love. Not the sort of love that people fall into or the passionate, chemical love that we can now find as easily as "swiping right." The love I'm talking about is the type of love John Paul was offering to his home country—the sacramental love of a broken Christ. This is the same type of sacrificial love Jesus demanded of each of his sheep. Biblical love is truth marinated in mercy.

You can find such love laid out in one of Jesus's most famous and powerful parables—that of the Good Samaritan (which we unpack in chapter 1). In that parable, Jesus reveals a four-step pattern of love:

1. *See: The **disposition** of our hearts toward mercy.* The Good Samaritan saw and "felt" mercy for the beaten enemy (part 1).
2. *Go: Getting close enough to others to **discover** their needs.* The Good Samaritan went to the beaten man in blessing and reconciliation (part 2).
3. *Do: Courageously **displacing** ourselves in service.* The Good Samaritan did what was just and right for the man (part 3).
4. *Endure: The **discipline** of mercy keeps us engaged.* The Good Samaritan was faithful, as he promised to return (part 4).

The first step—to see and feel—*is* the God Impulse. God's first impulse toward his fallen creation was mercy (see Eph. 2:4–5). Jesus said our first impulse toward our enemy should be mercy (see Luke 10:37). How much more should we respond in mercy toward those we love and toward fellow sin-

22

ners? The promise of this book is that when we take this first, often difficult step, the ligaments between us, God, and our neighbors will begin to reattach.

This personal pattern of love and connection that the Samaritan built for his wounded enemy is what we are calling a "bridge." This bridge of care, service, and resource brought the man from the brink of death to life. The Samaritan's promise to return confirms that this was more than a one-time "transactional" deed; it was possibly the promise of a future relationship. And so when we seek to imitate God and show his mercy and truth to the world, we must try to look at God's creation as God does—with overwhelming love and compassion and a willingness to personally bridge others as God has bridged us through Christ and the Holy Spirit. The God Impulse is meant to be the initial lens through which we see people and life—the impulse *to move toward* a hurting world in compassion and love.

The God Impulse can change me, you, and our world. Many Christians have a grid of truth through which they see the world; often they are judgmental and harsh. Most people have a grid of selfishness, and . . . well, we all know how that turns out. The God Impulse first asks what we can give to people, not what we can get. Instead of trying to figure out how we can make people a positive part of our story, the God Impulse asks the question, "What is *their* story?"

Join the journey of hope and healing. We can be relational, merciful, and faithful to God's truth. It's through this four-fold path of mercy that we can show the world the heart of God. We can connect people to him and to one another.

The Theological Conundrum about Mercy

In a church theology class, I studied authoritative texts that seemed to all but ignore mercy. Louis Berkhof's 184-page book *A Summary of Christian Doctrine* contains one sentence dedicated to mercy. Wayne Grudem's *Systematic Theology* (over five hundred thousand sold) includes one paragraph on mercy in over 1,200 pages. My concern is that if as God says, "All the paths of the LORD are mercy and truth," the "high view" of God and Scripture unwittingly has resulted in an understatement and under-teaching of mercy. Many Scriptures say, "the whole Law" is fulfilled via our mercy and love for our neighbor (e.g., Gal. 5:14 and 6:2). John sums it up well when he writes, "For whoever does not love their brother and sister, whom they have seen, cannot love God, whom they have not seen" (1 John 4:20–21 NIV). Thus, our horizontal love for one another proves the veracity of our vertical love for God.

No doubt that the central theology of the cross has played a role in this understatement. God's wrath and mercy met at the cross. The cross is the central manifestation of God's mercy in history for the forgiveness of the sins of the redeemed. The wrath of God was poured out on Christ; those who believe receive forgiveness for their past, present, and future sins. However, God continues to show us daily mercies and call us to be merciful to the poor and distressed, fellow sinners, and our enemies. Even today, God calls us to integrate biblical truth and mercy.

Catholics have taken almost an opposite tack. Mercy for the poor and distressed, sinners, and enemies is much more central to their theology. They may go too far, however, when they declare that "mercy is doctrine,"[7] effectively a trump card that invalidates much of revealed biblical truth about the character of God, including his justice and holiness. Mercy without justice is not the answer either.

It's not just religious groups that can lose the balance between truth and mercy. We find it in secular society too. And we find it in one of the thorniest and most tragic issues of our day: abortion.

Planned Parenthood celebrated its one hundredth anniversary in 2016. Its slogan is "care no matter what." In caring for women, they've lost sight of the fact that fetuses become human beings. More than fifty-six million abortions happen worldwide each year.[8]

Eighteen-year-old Maddi Ruckles might have been part of those statistics. The Christian teen, who kept a 4.0

grade point average at her Maryland Christian high school, got pregnant her senior year. She knew that merely showing up for class while pregnant would be a scandal. She was scared and ashamed. And so she considered doing something that, just months before, would've been unimaginable: she thought about getting an abortion.

"You're taught that it's wrong and you know that it's wrong," Maddi told CBS News. "And I never thought that I would consider it, but it was just the fear and what I've seen girls like me go through."[9]

What was the school's response? Maddi was banned from participating in her own graduation ceremony. Principal David R. Hobbs said that she was being punished "not because she is pregnant, but because she was immoral."[10]

"The best way to love her right now is to hold her accountable for her morality that began this situation," Hobbs wrote in a letter to parents.[11]

But was that really the best way to love her? What's the potential upshot of this purely truth-based stance, not just for Maddi, but for others? How many pregnant Christian girls might've heard her story and her school's reac-

tion and decided to have an abortion to save themselves the grief? Twenty? Thirty? Fifty? How many might've heard that story and saw a religion lacking in mercy and love?

Maddi eventually got her graduation ceremony. The organization Students for Life threw Maddi her very own party at a local Methodist church, complete with cap, gown, and diploma. "Abortion is a Christian problem," says Kristen Hawkins, president of Students for Life. "Over half of women who have abortions identify as Christians and more than 40 percent of those are regular churchgoers."[12]

How many of those regular churchgoers would've kept their babies had their own communities shown just a little more mercy?

The world is looking for our leaders to model truth marinated in mercy.

So many other issues, such as treatment of refugees, immigration, and gender and sexual identity, are a standoff because truth folks and mercy folks are not able to integrate two critical sides of God's character. Psalm 85:10 says that when "mercy and truth are met together; righteousness and peace have kissed each other" (KJV).

1

The God Impulse

When we are on the receiving end of mercy, we experience the ultimate sense of safety. What does it feel like to be safe?

A friend of mine tells the story of when he was just a little boy. Occasionally, his parents took him to dinners and get-togethers, and sometimes, if the party went late, my friend—all of five or six years old then—curled up on the carpet and fell asleep.

Later that night, the boy opened his eyes and saw that he was in the back seat of the family's car, trees sprinting past as the moon raced beside. He shut his eyes again and soon felt the car crunch into their gravel driveway. The engine stopped. The car door opened. And then he felt the big, strong hands of his father pull him up and out of the seat and swaddle him in his arms. His father's walk felt like a rocking chair as they made their way inside.

For my friend, that's what safety feels like: To be five again and feel your father's arms wrap around you. To be carried home. Sometimes he simply pretended to fall asleep, just to feel those arms again.

My friend was lucky. Too many of us have not had this experience.

My father died when I was nine years old. Too many nights I remember hearing my mother crying over her unimaginable loss. Eventually, my mother remarried, but my stepfather was cold and strict, more likely to dole out harsh words than grace me with a hug. Worse, they would fight constantly, often about money. I unpack more of my story in my book *The God Guarantee*, but here I simply want to emphasize that my home was filled with stress, anger, and recriminations. That safety? That warmth my friend felt in a father's arms? Those things weren't much a part of my life. They were mysteries. At the time, they might've well been myths.

Our Need for Merciful "Arms"

We live in a place of pain.

Spin the globe and point, and you'll find it. Hunger in Sierra Leone. Human trafficking in Thailand. Murders in Mexico. Poverty in Atlanta. Sad stories stuff our newspapers and fill our Facebook feeds every day of the week.

How many children go to bed hungry and scared every night? How many adults? The need is overwhelming. The hurt is felt in every ghetto and borough, every neighborhood and street.

Yes, some of us are better off than others. If you're reading this now, chances are you're not doing too badly by the world's sad standards. You don't worry about where your next meal will come from. You have a place to live. Perhaps you're successful. Comfortable. Maybe you even describe yourself as happy.

But we all carry the scars of old wounds. And no matter what station we've reached in life, we all can feel scared, insecure, and alone. I know I do. I can have positive outcomes in life, but I still feel insecure and unworthy sometimes. I feel scared. Part of me will always feel like a frightened little boy longing to be held.

Maybe we all yearn to feel those strong arms around us, brushing away our fear and protecting us from danger. How we need to be lifted up out of our sorrow and pain. How desperately we yearn to hear someone tell us that we're loved. That we're safe. That everything will be all right.

What do we need to feel when we're hurting and hungry? When we're lost and frightened? Even when we've made mistakes?

We need those arms. We need to feel safe and protected—even when we deserve those arms the least.

Those arms are a metaphor for love. When we feel like we deserve love—when we feel worthy or successful or particularly cute, like my friend was when he was five years old—most of us may be able to find those arms easily enough. It's simple to find love when we're lovable. But ironically, we most need that love when we're *not* lovable—when we're feeling wretched and ugly, when we know we're unworthy, and when our failures are laid out for the entire world to see. *That's* when we most need those arms to hold, comfort, and protect us. And that is so often when they're difficult—sometimes impossible—to find.

In India, many believe a huge group of people are literally unworthy of being held. They're called "untouchables," and even contact with the shadow of an untouchable is thought to make you unclean. I've spent years trying to help them. Many others have too. But among many of their own people, they're considered truly unlovable.

India's not alone. In every country, every stratum of society, we find people whom others treat as unlovable, untouchable. The poor. Addicts. Sons and daughters who've shamed their family name. Friends who've hurt us. Sometimes we salve our guilt by writing a check to a needy cause, but rarely do we look those we're helping in the eye. And other times, if we've been hurt or made angry by a personal "untouchable," we do nothing at all—except maybe cross to the other side of the street.

But they don't need our money—and they certainly don't need our scorn, as much as they need something else: love. Pure, generous love.

And what do you call love given to the unlovable? Those arms wrapped around the untouchable?

I call it mercy. And you know what? God does too.

God's Illustration of Mercy: The Good Samaritan

One story illustrates the God Impulse more than any other: the parable of the Good Samaritan (see Luke 10:25–37).

The parable itself is actually a response to a question. A lawyer walked up to Jesus and, according to verse 25, decided to "test" him. "Teacher, what shall I do to inherit eternal life?" the man asked. Jesus answered the man with more questions: "What is written in the Law? How do you read it?" (v. 26).

The lawyer gave an answer that any Sunday school teacher would be proud of. "You shall love the Lord your God with all your heart and with all your soul and with all your strength and with all your mind, and your neighbor as yourself" (v. 27). Jesus told the lawyer that he was absolutely right. "Do this, and you will live" (v. 28).

But the lawyer wasn't done. He tried to "justify himself"—to pat himself on the back for caring for all the good, decent people like himself—and asked, "And who is my neighbor?" (v. 29).

Again, Jesus didn't answer directly. Instead, he began his story, unfolding a tale about a traveler waylaid on one of the most notorious roads in ancient Judea.

> A man was going down from Jerusalem to Jericho, and he fell among robbers, who stripped him and beat him and departed, leaving him half dead. (v. 30)

The road from Jerusalem to Jericho was infamous in Jesus's day, and even though Jericho was to the north of Jerusalem, travelers literally went *down* to Jericho, as in downhill: Jerusalem is about 2,500 feet above sea level, while Jericho is more than 800 feet below. The road was hot, dry, and incredibly dangerous. A key pass is still known in Arabic as *Tal'at ed-Damm*, which translates into "ascent of blood" or "the bloody way." Many experts suspect the pass earned its name because of the constant threat of violent bandits and that Jesus's traveler—if he had been a real person—would've likely been attacked here.[1]

Despite its dangers, the road was a popular artery for commercial traffic. Caravans, pilgrims, and Roman troops regularly traversed the eighteen-mile pass. So Jesus's audience wouldn't have been surprised that the traveler had company on the road. Jesus continued:

> Now by chance a priest was going down that road, and when he saw him he passed by on the other side. So likewise a Levite, when he came to the place and saw him, passed by on the other side. (vv. 31–32)

Priests and Levites were the two most prominent religious orders in Jesus's times—people who you'd think would be the most likely to help. So why didn't they? Scholars have pointed to a number of possible reasons, some of which we'll explore in greater detail later in this book. But briefly, it's possible they thought the traveler was already dead. Both priests and Levites were made ritually "unclean" if they touched a dead body. Perhaps they didn't take the time for a closer look.

Or maybe they saw that the traveler was alive but worried that he was bait for a trap. Martin Luther King Jr. subscribed to this in his 1968 "I've Been to the Mountaintop" speech:

> It's possible that they felt that the man on the ground was merely faking, and he was acting like he had been robbed and hurt in order to seize them over there, lure them there for quick and easy seizure. And so the first question that the priest asked, the first question that the Levite asked was, "If I stop to help this man, what will happen to me?"[2]

Or it could be that they simply didn't want to be bothered. But, according to Jesus, someone *did* stop.

> But a Samaritan, as he journeyed, came to where he was, and when he saw him, he had compassion. He went to him and bound up his wounds, pouring on oil and wine. Then

he set him on his own animal and brought him to an inn and took care of him. And the next day he took out two denarii and gave them to the innkeeper, saying, "Take care of him, and whatever more you spend, I will repay you when I come back." (vv. 33–35)

By definition, a Samaritan was simply a person who lived in a region known as Samaria, just north of Judea and south of Galilee. But to Jesus's Jewish audience, the word was freighted with provocative meaning. Jews and Samaritans *hated* each other. The Bible tells us that the two ethnic groups had "no dealings" (John 4:9 NASB) with each other, and when Jews wanted to slander Jesus, they asked him, "Are we not right in saying that you are a Samaritan and have a demon?" (John 8:48). For them, being a Samaritan and being demon-possessed was practically the same thing.

Samaritans were considered idol worshipers and defilers. They intermarried and profaned Jerusalem's sacred temple by scattering human bones around the sanctuary.[3] And truth be told, the Samaritans harbored no love for Jews either. Giving a Samaritan the role of a hero, as Jesus did, must've felt truly scandalous to his Jewish questioner. It would've been akin to switching out the Samaritan with a Palestinian today. Or in Rwanda, just after the country's genocide, illustrating the story using a Hutu and a Tutsi.

Or imagine, if you will, a similar scene on the streets of Atlanta. A conservative Christian is robbed, beaten, and left half dead. His Bible lies by his side. Maybe he's wearing a ripped shirt supporting the local Republican candidate or proclaiming his opposition to same-sex marriage. There's no question of who the man is and what he stands for. And who comes to his rescue? A man just leaving a local pride rally, carrying a rainbow flag and wearing a dress. The man stoops down, bandages the Christian's wounds, puts the man's arm around his own shoulders, and carries him inside to safety, promising to care for him until he recovers.

That's the sort of meeting Jesus had in mind when he made the Samaritan the protagonist in his parable.

With that, Jesus ended his parable, turned to the lawyer, and asked which of the three was a neighbor to the man attacked by the robbers, to which the man replied, "The one who showed him mercy." And then Jesus said to him, "Go, and do likewise" (v. 37).

In this book, we will cover that mercy is for not only victims but also perpetrators. This is why it is both complex and controversial. So our mercy needs to go beyond the widows and orphans most of us have a natural impulse to help. It needs to extend to the broken; the people who don't seem to deserve it. Even to our enemies. And somehow, Jesus conveyed in one short story how we can show mercy to all those people who deserve it.

I'll be drawing your attention to several passages in Jesus's story of the Good Samaritan throughout this book, but let's begin with one easily missed: "Then [the Good Samaritan] put the man on his own donkey" (v. 34 NIV).

Picture that for a moment—the Samaritan with this bloodied, broken traveler. The Samaritan bandaged the man's wounds and then reached out and picked him up, holding the bloody man in his arms as he helped the traveler up onto his donkey. It's a moment of intimacy—a moment of powerful, caring connection. It reminds me of my friend at the beginning of this chapter being picked up, held, and finally, carried home.

Finding Mercy

In this book, I want to take you on a journey of *mercy*, uncovering the power and beauty locked inside that small, two-syllable word. I'll unveil a process—a pattern of love, God's impulse—that will change us, our relationships, and maybe even the world.

But the first step in the journey is fully understanding what the word even means and why it's so important. Because even in Christianity—a faith that talks about and depends on mercy like no other—the word isn't understood very well.

A pastor in Atlanta recently defined mercy as "not getting the punishment I deserve." And I think that's how many of us define it—as judgment withheld. Accused criminals throw themselves on the mercy of the court. Conquering armies might show mercy on the conquered. In Christianity, we believe that God, in forgiving our sins, shows *us* mercy. We deserve death but we receive forgiveness instead.

And to be sure, that whole "not getting the punishment I deserve" is part of mercy. But it's more than that. Much, much more. The word is absolutely central to God's character. In fact, the word defines him.

When Moses smashed the original stone tablets of the commandments because of the people's rebellion, God came down to replace them, calling himself "a God merciful and gracious, slow to anger, and abounding in steadfast love" (Exod. 34:6). David echoes those words verbatim in Psalm 103. Paul writes that God is "rich in mercy" (Eph. 2:4–5 NIV). And when Jesus gave his disciples instructions for how to live, he pointed to his heavenly Father as the very best example of how to live a life full of compassion and kindness. "Be merciful, just as your Father is merciful," Christ said (Luke

6:36 NIV). Repeatedly, the King James Version of the Bible talks about God's "tender mercies" that are given to us daily.

Yes, God's mercy is about him being slow to anger, as it says in Exodus. But it goes beyond that. This core attribute extends to God's steadfast love. He's not just withholding the punishment we deserve. He's giving us the love we so desperately need.

Imagine for a moment that God's a father, waiting for a kid who missed his curfew. When the child finally comes home, what does mercy look like in that moment? Some might imagine God with his arms crossed and a scowl on his face. "Oh, it's all right," he'd say, looking at the child's crestfallen face. "Go on up to bed."

But in my understanding of mercy—the biblical understanding, I believe—God doesn't just tap his foot. He rushes to the door and embraces the boy, asking him if he's scared or hurt or if something happened. He wants to wrap us in his arms and know the story behind that missed curfew. He's not concerned about the broken law as much as he's concerned about *us*. And that is a beautiful thing.

In his outstanding book *Ministries of Mercy*, Tim Keller writes, "Grace has to do with man's merits, but mercy has to do with man's misery. Theologians have discerned that God's mercy . . . is that aspect of His nature which moves Him to relieve suffering and misery."[4]

When God is being merciful, he's not merely holding back his wrath; he's extending a hand to us. He lifts us up. He takes us up in his arms. He protects us and heals us. When we're at our absolute worst, God is at his most merciful. He loves us so much that he almost can't help himself.

That's what the God Impulse is. It's rushing into the breach to help and heal and hold us when we need it most. It's the understanding that when we become a bridge to others in need, we profoundly change their lives for good.

God doesn't take us into his arms because it's his job and he must. Every fiber of his infinite being is geared toward loving, nurturing, and protecting his creation. We saw it when he placed his mark on Cain. When he made his pact with Abraham. When he sent his only Son to teach us, heal us, and eventually die for us.

We see God's mercy illustrated in many of Jesus's parables, especially that of the Good Samaritan. God has been that Samaritan to those of us who've accepted him—those of us who can call ourselves his children. We've been the wounded traveler, beaten by sin, grief, and doubt. We've felt God's arms around us. And we'll feel those arms again someday in a much more tangible way—when God lifts us up and carries us home.

Those of us who call ourselves Christians know what mercy feels like, even if we don't always use the word.

And because we know God's mercy, God asks us to turn around and show that mercy to others. To wrap our arms around a hurting world and offer comfort. Healing. Safety.

"Be merciful, just as your Father is merciful," Jesus told us. But that's easier said than done. If we're honest with ourselves, we rarely feel God's impulse. It comes only with practice.

Risky Business

Monica stared at me across the table in a hotel meeting room. Her face was tight and pale. Her mouth was pinched, her eyes narrowed in anger. I could see her hands were trembling—not from fear, I guessed, but from fury. At me.

How different this felt from our first meeting a few years earlier. She'd charmed me then with her business savvy and drive. She was a rising star in the travel industry we both worked in, and I'd almost hired her. Instead, she accepted a job with one of our competitors.

She became the only woman partner in the business and performed admirably.

But that competitor was in deep trouble now, hemorrhaging millions of dollars every year. They began cutting costs and denied her money that was owed to her. She quit and sued the company for what she was due.

My company had finalized the purchase of the business she had worked for. In the transaction, we assumed certain liabilities and lawsuits, including the one from Monica. She now was across from me—and had a lot to say.

For twenty minutes she pounded me with facts, her pain and anger palpable in every word. "I was the only woman shareholder! *The only one!* I was marginalized. My reputation was hurt."

I sat there in silence.

It wasn't my fault that Monica had lost her stock; she'd filed the lawsuit against the company I was buying. I was, technically, innocent. But when you buy a company, you buy all of its baggage too—faulty structure, troublesome employees, outstanding lawsuits. Maybe what happened to Monica hadn't been my fault, but it was now my responsibility. I could allow the lawsuit to run its course and let the courts decide what was right, or I could take a different tack.

Finally, I said, "Everything you said is right. The company is wrong. I am sorry. We need to determine how much money we owe you."

Monica sat for a moment, perhaps surprised by my honesty. Then her eyes filled with tears. When she opened her mouth to speak, her lower lip quivered.

"What would you do if you were me?" she asked.

We sat together and talked about it. We talked about her righteous anger, her understandable pain. And then we talked about God. That God of mercy. That God of healing. That God who picks us up and carries us home.

The meeting began in confrontation. It ended in confession and prayer.

After we prayed, she stood up and walked toward the door. As her hand reached for the doorknob, I spoke again.

"Monica," I said, "what do you want to do? About the lawsuit?"

She paused. "Jack, what do you think is fair?"

I thought about it and then gave her a dollar amount— one with seven figures. That, I suggested, would be fair compensation.

"That's fine," she said and walked out.

A few years later, I was raising money for a charity organization I work with that helps people escape bonded slavery in India. One day we got a check for $20,000 for the charity. It came from the charitable trust Monica had created from the money that had been owed to her.

God desires for mercy to be shown for sinners. When we bridge broken, sinful people or purchase broken companies, mercy is always costly. It is messy business. The company I purchased had sinned against Monica. When I bought it, I "assumed" that sin. When I confessed the sin and agreed with Monica, she then was merciful in agreeing to settle the lawsuit. The amount she received was generous, but in a lawsuit, "bad facts," like those that existed here, can result in large awards. I was generous with her—but fair. And my generosity gave her permission to be generous too. That's the beauty of mercy: the bridges build on each other.

Imperfect Impulses

The God Impulse isn't natural to us. Not really. If God's first impulse is to wrap us in his arms no matter how unlovable and untouchable we may seem, our first impulse is to wrap our hands into fists and start pounding at whatever might get in our way.

When someone hurts us, we want to hurt them back. When someone makes us uncomfortable, we want to get away from that discomfort in the quickest and easiest way possible. Like the priest and Levite in the Good Samaritan parable, we're inclined to cross to the other side of the street. It's human nature.

Our world tells us to get stuff *for* ourselves, not give *of* ourselves. In fact, showing mercy is often seen as weakness. Feed the poor? *They should work for a living*, we think. Care for the widows? *Who has time for that?* We're obsessed with getting and keeping *what's ours*. Everybody else can fend for themselves. Instead of solving problems in a merciful, healing way, we handle our slights with lawsuits. More than 1.1 million lawyers are kept at work in the United States— one attorney for every three hundred people, the most per capita on earth.[5]

We're a selfish people, and it seems as though we're getting more so all the time. The business world—the world I'm most familiar with—can be particularly unmerciful. It's predicated on a far more Darwinian "survival of the fittest" mode of operation than of anything predicated on God's curious calculus.

And yet I think that even in the business world, we find elements that can illustrate mercy and help us better show mercy to others. Because here's the crazy thing about mercy: it's not just the *right* course of action, it's often the *smart* course of action. Showing mercy opens doors that would otherwise stay sealed shut. Mercy precipitates actions that would be inconceivable without it. We'll unpack some of those lessons as the book goes on, but for now it's important to remember one thing: mercy feeds on itself, and in so doing, it has the power to feed the world.

In the situation with Monica, mercy was at work. God, in his mercy, showed me the first step of mercy itself—his own impulse: to *see*. To look someone in the eyes, to feel the need in those eyes, and like the Good Samaritan, try to make it a little better. Because of that impulse, what could've been a soul-sapping business-as-usual meeting turned into something more profound. And because of Monica's mercy toward me, we could both walk away from that meeting smiling.

Because Monica had seen the God Impulse at work, she came to a better understanding of God himself. And when she had the opportunity to show another sort of mercy to some hurting, enslaved people in India, she took it.

What's Their Story?

Monica's story illustrates a key attribute of mercy—one so often overlooked in our more traditional understanding of the word. I didn't truly understand how buying the company had impacted Monica when we first sat down to talk. How could I know without having spoken to her? When I understood the entire story, it was obvious something needed to change. I knew I needed to offer an olive branch.

To be truly merciful, we have to be willing to look someone in the eye. To kneel down beside him. To get to know them. To hold them. *We need to hear their story.* When we're willing to do that, we may discover (to our shock) that folks seemingly "undeserving" of our mercy deserve it much more than we think.

I'm amazed how often we don't take the time to listen to other people and try to understand what's really going on in their lives. And I'm surprised at myself sometimes, because I can be as guilty of this as anyone. We try not to involve ourselves. Even when we're trying to be merciful, we keep that mercy at arm's length. We write checks to ministries or organizations that get their hands dirty instead of getting dirty ourselves. So much cleaner that way. Safer. It's easier to give some money to a soup kitchen than invite a homeless man to dinner.

But remember, mercy is a manifestation of love. And what do we do when we show love to someone? *We get involved.* A check, no matter how generous, is not a good substitute for those arms of affection.

A Snapshot of Mercy

Members of the Ku Klux Klan stood on a street in Ann Arbor, Michigan, in full regalia—the white sheets, the pointed hoods. Their very presence on that day in June 1996 was a symbol of hate; a history of burning crosses and lynchings; a terrible reminder of a twisted, broken, and all-too-merciless world. Across the way stood hundreds of protestors shouting down the KKK with righteous anger.[6]

Suddenly, one of the protesters announced over a megaphone that there was a "Klansman in the crowd." The protesters whirled around and saw Albert McKeel Jr., a white man wearing a T-shirt with a confederate flag on it. A tattoo of the Nazi SS symbol was branded on his arm. And he was in the middle of the protesters: for him, it was enemy territory.

Was he part of the KKK demonstration? No one knows, even more than twenty years later. He didn't have a chance to speak. Instead, he took off running as protesters ran after him.

"Kill the Nazi!" some hollered as McKeel was pulled to the ground. Kicks and fists began to rain down on the man, the crowd screaming for blood.

But then Keshia Thomas—an eighteen-year-old black woman who'd come to protest the KKK—pushed through the crowd and crouched beside the man, protecting his body with hers, wrapping him in her arms.

"I knew what it was like to be hurt," Thomas later told the BBC. "The many times that that happened, I wish someone would have stood up for me."[7]

What is safety?

For McKeel that day, it meant Keshia Thomas holding him.

What does it mean to be merciful?

For Thomas that day, it was sheltering a man—a man who might just hate her—from a crowd's merciless blows.

Thomas was, and is, a woman of faith. And when she talks about the incident, she frames it in religious terms. "When they dropped him to the ground," she said, "it felt like two angels had lifted my body up and laid me down."[8]

Did this act of mercy change McKeel? We may never know. He never spoke about the incident, and he died a few years ago, taking his opinion to the grave.

But it did change others.

Months later, a man recognized Thomas in a coffee shop. He walked up to her and said thanks for what she did that day. "That was my dad," he explained.[9]

When McKeel died, the son called Thomas to tell her—and he put his twelve-year-old sister on the phone. The girl thanked Thomas herself, telling her that if it hadn't been for Thomas's mercy that day, she might never have been born.

> "When I heard that, I thought this was the future and the past of what peace has created," Thomas said. "The real accomplishment of all this to me is to know that his son and daughter don't share the same views. History didn't repeat itself. That's what gives me hope that the world can get better from generation to generation."[10]

Teri Gunderson wasn't in Ann Arbor that day in 1996. She never met Thomas. But the woman keeps a picture of her anyway. For her, Thomas has become a symbol of hope—a manifestation, I'd say, of the God Impulse. She told the BBC: "The voice in my head says something like this: 'If she could protect a man [like that], I can show kindness to this person.' And with that encouragement, I do act with more kindness. I don't know her, but since then I am more kind."[11]

The God Impulse is hard. Sometimes it's hard to feel, and it can even be harder to follow. It's countercultural. It's the opposite of what the world tells us to be. I'm sure some critics will say that mercy's naive. Silly. Antiquated. It won't change anything.

But it can. Oh, it can.

Mercy wraps us in its arms. It protects us. Nurtures us. Heals us. Saves us. And it's only when we learn how to follow God's example—God's impulse—that we can begin to save the world. We have seen how the arms of mercy can wrap around the hurting and helpless, fellow sinners, and even our enemies. We can, in our own special ways, pick up others and carry them home.

This pattern of love—this God Impulse—is not easy to follow. In some ways, it goes against our own instincts. Author Anne Lamott says,

> An open, merciful heart is a setup for pain, shame, and being mocked. We are not stupid: welcome to Vengeance World. . . . Just to hear the words *mercy* or *merciful* can transform the whole day, because, as the old saying says, the soul rejoices in hearing what it already knows. We know mercy is always our salvation.[12]

Whereas the God Impulse of mercy is difficult, it is *possible*. And I promise that it has the power to change not only the lives of those who accept that mercy but also those who give it. Indeed, it has the power to change the world.

God's Pattern of Love for You: His Impulse

Our impulse toward others often mirrors what we think God's impulse is toward us. Isn't it exciting that he understands our fears, weaknesses, and limitations? Psalm 103:14 says, "For he knows our frame; he remembers that we are dust." Just think, he created humankind from dust and breathed into you and me. Please know that no matter how you are feeling today, he can breathe hope and create a new future for you. His impulse toward you is kindness. Reach out to him and thank him.

PART 1

SEE:

The Disposition of Mercy

SEEING AND FEELING GOD'S IMPULSE

And when he saw him,
he had compassion. (Luke 10:33)

2

Eight Seconds to See

I came to Christ halfway around the world, in Australia. I'd never seen love like I found in a small community of worshipers called Richmond Temple. I'd never felt the sort of mercy they showed me and others. All my life, I'd fought feelings of insecurity. All my life, I'd tried to live up to unseen expectations. Here, finally, with these people and with this strange new faith, I'd found a real home. A shelter from the storm. An inn along the dangerous road of life we all walk.

And with Jesus new in my soul, I began to look for an opportunity to show that same sort of love and mercy to someone else.

It didn't take long.

I remember driving in Melbourne one evening and seeing a man perhaps one hundred yards away from me. He was staggering down the street. Dirty. Probably homeless. But I believed—I *sensed*, really—that the Lord wanted me to drive up beside him.

So I did. I pulled up beside him and stopped. I leaned over and looked out of the passenger-side window at him.

A red, ragged gash was torn across the man's forehead. Blood ran from the wound and trickled past his eye. Dirt was dried on his face, turning it a deep tan color. His cheekbones pushed against his skin. Scruff covered his neck.

Without a word, he opened the door and got in.

I wasn't expecting God's prompting to have such an immediate response. Maybe another day, I wouldn't have even seen this man. I would've barreled on down the road—head down, heart calloused.

But on this day, I saw.

I was headed to a get-together with some Christian friends, and this stranger, this new friend, came with me. I didn't hesitate; I knew the man—dirty, bleeding, and hungry—would be accepted and welcomed just as he was. Just as I had been welcomed by them the way I was. I led the man inside the house, where my friends surrounded him and immediately took him to the kitchen to wash out his wound.

We bandaged up his head. We gave him something to eat. We smiled and talked with him as he sat with us—our unexpected guest.

I can't say where that man is today, but I have a vivid memory of what can happen when my eyes are open and I lift up my head to see what God is doing. My hope is that it's a memory for the wounded man as well.

Humans versus Goldfish

Eight seconds.

That's the average attention span of a human today, according to a study from Microsoft. Researchers say that *goldfish* are more attentive than we are.[1]

Of course, goldfish don't have social media to distract them. Back in 2000—before Facebook or the iPhone or any of the other technological distractions that dominate our world today—we could typically concentrate on something for twelve seconds before our minds began to wander. In the space of just fifteen years, our own incredible advances and frenetic societal pace have conspired, paradoxically, to make us *dumber*.[2] After all, the ability to concentrate is key in our ability to create and achieve. I bet that you looked out the window, checked your social media status, or thought about what to have for dinner before you even finished this paragraph. I did all three in the time it took to write it.

The next benchmark in our dwindling attention spans? Perhaps the fruit fly with its three-second attention span. This insect has notoriously lax concentration, and given that most fruit flies live between forty and fifty days, perhaps that's understandable. But scientists believe the human brain and the fruit fly brain have some commonalities—so much so, in fact, that scientists are studying the flies to better understand why we humans suffer from autism and attention deficit hyperactivity disorder. In fact, researchers found that giving fruit flies Ritalin improved their attention spans.[3]

We can see the impact of this eight-second attention span everywhere in our culture. Movies are more over the top than ever in an effort to keep us engaged. Forget thirty-second ad spots. YouTube advertisers are cramming their pitches into *five-second spaces*, trying to tell the story of their company before viewers push the "skip" button.[4] Nightly newscast? Forget it. Most folks get their news in short Facebook blasts or short Twitter missives.

This enemy, hurry, contributes to the lack of mercy in our culture as well. It's a sad truth that, in an age when technology allows us to connect with more people than ever before, our connections are shallow and fleeting. We sure look at a lot of stuff these days, but we don't really *see* much of anything.

Our inability to see the suffering around us and feel empathy for that suffering when we do see it prevents us from embracing God's impulse toward mercy. Thus, seeing is the first step we have to take toward that impulse. Our first "on-ramp" to this merciful bridge, if you will, is to have the disposition or inclination to see. We can only have this if we realize it is our natural tendency not to.

Think again of the Good Samaritan. Before he could bandage up the traveler's wounds and take him to the inn, what had to happen? He had to *see* him. He had to feel an inkling to help. "And when he saw him, he had compassion" (Luke 10:33).

If Jesus's traveler in the Good Samaritan story was waylaid today, the priest and Levite might've never looked up from their phones.

The Upside-Down Kingdom

David's famous twenty-third Psalm begins like this:

> The LORD is my shepherd; I shall not want
> He makes me lie down in green pastures.
> He leads me beside still waters.
> He restores my soul. (vv. 1–3)

Those green pastures and still waters feel a world away from our own, don't they? We struggle to find that sense of peace, to discover that merciful womb God provides, and to somehow provide that womb for others. And yet, it was a challenge for David too, wasn't it? His time, in a way, was just as chaotic as ours. However, he experienced the ability to rest in God.

In this chapter, we'll talk about some of the challenges our eight-second attention span presents to showing and giving mercy, including how our culture makes it difficult to truly see the need around us. More importantly, we'll unpack how to overcome that chaos. We'll learn how to best follow the example of the Good Samaritan to see and feel.

We have to. This on-ramp to mercy is important not only for us to love others well but also for us to heal ourselves.

It's a paradox. If we want to experience the healing balm of mercy, one of the ways we do so is by extending that mercy to others. I understand that. But our world is full of paradoxes.

We're more connected than we've ever been, but most of us feel more alone than ever.

Most of us carry all the knowledge of the world in our pockets, but we can't concentrate on any of it long enough to make a difference.

We get directions from our phones with just a couple of clicks or a word or two, but we're more lost than ever.

Now, in this area of mercy, we face our biggest test: we're asked to give away the most precious things we have—our time and attention—to others. In addition, we need to give up our sensibilities—sometimes our desire for justice or revenge. Mercy takes us down that dreaded path of forgiveness from the heart. We like to read stories about amazing acts of forgiveness shown by others but not create acts of our own. And yet when we give those things that are so valuable to us, we can find purpose for ourselves and others.

In October 2006, Terri Roberts's son, Charles, shot ten young Amish girls, killing five of them, at their one-room schoolhouse in Nickel Mines, Pennsylvania. It was one of the most horrific crimes imaginable—one precipitated, according to the *New York Times*, by a twenty-year-old grudge.[5] You can imagine how the parents of those girls must've felt toward their daughters' killer—indeed, the killer's entire family. Such a crime would've been, for most of us, unforgivable.

However, these grieving parents chose to *forgive*—to show mercy to Terri during her own time of grief and horror and sorrow. Some of the victims' families attended Charles's funeral (he committed suicide after shooting the girls) and comforted her and her husband. Terri cares for the most seriously injured girl every week and has become a vessel of mercy and service to others. Her advice to those suffering unimaginable loss? "Ask God to provide new things in your lives, new things to focus on," she says. "That does not take the place of what is lost. But it can give us a hope and a future."[6]

The time we spend focusing on others can, paradoxically, provide that pasture that God takes us to, the still waters we lie beside. When we restore others, we restore . . . us.

But that requires an important first step in our pattern of love: the ability to see what needs to be restored.

Seeing Like God Does

While bats rely on their sense of hearing and sharks depend on their sense of smell, we humans lean on our sense of sight. We filter the world through our eyes, so perhaps it's not too surprising that God would focus on this sense too.

But God often tells us that we don't use this primary sense as we really should—particularly when it comes to seeing what's really important. We find the phrase "seeing but not perceiving" in ten books in the Bible, both in the Old and New Testaments. With that kind of coverage, it's clear that most of us struggle with being shortsighted.

I can relate to this. So often I can walk through a room and not "see" much of anything (much to the chagrin of my wife). The room could be cluttered with unfamiliar stuff and I wouldn't notice. The furniture might be rearranged and I might not detect anything really different—until, that is, I tried to sit down in my favorite easy chair.

I think many of us are like that. We might drive to work the same way every morning for months before we notice a new building. "When did *that* get there?" we might ask. It might be days before we realize our rosebushes are in bloom. We feel like we know our homes, our towns, and our worlds pretty well. And so we stop truly seeing them.

We can be spiritually shortsighted as well. The apostle Paul, who some believe had poor natural vision, said he saw spirituality as "in a mirror dimly" (1 Cor. 13:12).

No matter how long we walk with Christ, that glass won't clear up entirely. We'll always be learning new things, new facets of God's character. But our spiritual vision does get better, although not perfect, with time. I've often thought that new Christians should be told right up front that, "Yes, you have the capacity to see with new spiritual eyes, but it will take you years before you'll be able to see well."

So what do we need to see more clearly? What sort of spiritual glasses can we make to help us see the world the way God would like us to see it?

When you go to an optometrist, they'll typically make you look at an eye chart through a series of lenses. "Can you see better through lens number one? Or"—they'll say as they snap a new choice into view—"lens number two? How about three . . . or four?"

In God's kingdom, it seems like Jesus and the Bible's authors wanted us to look at the world through the lenses of some surprising people—people who, in our world, often don't count for much. These folks, often afterthoughts in our own worldly kingdom, are princes and princesses in God's kingdom. Here are a few people who are like lenses that help us see those who are great in God's kingdom:

- *The poor in spirit.* "Blessed are the poor in spirit, for theirs is the kingdom of heaven" (Matt. 5:3 NIV).
- *The literal poor.* "Blessed are you who are poor, for yours is the kingdom of God" (Luke 6:20 NIV).
- *Children.* "Truly, I say to you, unless you turn and become like children, you will never enter the kingdom of heaven. Whoever humbles himself like this child is the greatest in the kingdom of heaven" (Matt. 18:3–4).
- *Servants.* "The greatest among you shall be your servant. Whoever exalts himself will be humbled, and whoever humbles himself will be exalted" (Matt. 23:11–12).
- *Slaves.* "Instead, whoever wants to become great among you must be your servant, and whoever wants to be first must be your slave" (Matt. 20:26–27 NIV).
- *Those who learn and teach the Bible.* "But whoever practices and teaches these commands will be called great in the kingdom of heaven" (Matt. 5:19 HCSB).

- *Small things.* "One who is faithful in a very little is also faithful in much, and one who is dishonest in a very little is also dishonest in much" (Luke 16:10).
- *Enemies.* "But I say to you, Love your enemies and pray for those who persecute you" (Matt. 5:44).

We could probably include more people on this list. Maybe a lot more. But these lenses seemed apparent to me. Did you notice how we often have a tendency to look past many of these people or things? We cannot be "great" in God's kingdom if we do not see the people and understand the things he calls great.

It's natural, I suppose. It's how the world trains us.

In business, I've been taught to value certain elements and people based on their value to the world. I've learned to see how "significant" something is to the success and well-being of whatever I'm working on. The rich make businesses click. The powerful grease their wheels. A business's "friends" will buy the product and advocate for other people to buy it too. These are "significant" people in the realm of business. The poor? The children? The servants? Not hardly.

I don't think these dynamics are isolated to the business world. Whatever endeavors you're involved with, you probably well know that "success"—worldly success, at least—is dependent on who you know. The richer and more powerful they are, the better.

But look at God's list again. It tells us that the poor are blessed, not the rich. The servants will be greater, not the masters. The enemies should be prayed for. Each of these things is humble, small, or wholly unexpected. It's the nature of God's kingdom.

We can feel the wisdom and beauty when we look through these lenses. In personal relationships, so often the small things count the most: A gentle gesture. A well-placed word. Washing dishes for your spouse without being asked and when it's not your turn. A visit to a bedside during a time of need. How you handle the small things can really communicate love and care.

I know how I feel when God answers a small prayer of mine: blessed. I know he heard me. He cares for me. And to a seemingly small thing, he says yes. Such love can bring tears to our eyes.

Many of us have probably heard the saying "Learn to love what God loves and hate what he hates." Well, here's what God loves: the poor, the children, the slaves, the small. All the people and things the world encourages us to ignore, God wants us to see. That's what makes the Good Samaritan story so powerful; he saw and responded to the beaten man who was, technically, his enemy. He reached down to help someone who was poor and vulnerable.

He not only saw what was happening, but he also did something about it. He knew he had to. Because even though he was a Samaritan—outside God's "chosen people" at the time—he looked through the lenses God wanted him to see through.

So often we don't. We can understand why God revisits this area again and again: *we see, but we do not perceive.*

True Sight

Not many Christians truly perceived the horrors of AIDS in Africa in 2002. It was the year after 9/11, and most of us were still reeling from the aftermath. So many other needs seemed to fill our line of sight, and Africa was so far away. Some Christians even thought that AIDS was, in fact, a punishment from God. They couldn't see (or didn't want to see) that the disease was devastating families across the continent, killing countless mothers and fathers and leaving their innocent children orphaned.

But in 2002, Kay Warren—wife of Rick Warren, founding pastor of California's massive Saddleback Church and author of *The Purpose Driven Life*, published that same year—read an article about the AIDS crisis in Africa. And her whole world was turned upside down.

The article unpacked the tragedy in excruciating detail. The pictures were so graphic, according to *Christianity Today*, that Kay couldn't even look at them.[7] She had to cover her eyes, and she read the story through the cracks between her fingers. According to the article Kay read, AIDS had orphaned *twelve million* children in Africa—more than the population of Seoul or Cairo.[8]

Kay was struck by the terrible, unfolding tragedy. The story pulled at her heart. She knew she had to act.

"I just knew that Kay Warren, Christian, had to say yes to God," she said during a special webcast in 2010. "From there I began to learn and study. God just broke my heart. He just wiped me out. There is not a day that goes by that I don't cry over what I've learned and what I've seen."[9]

She said back during that 2010 telecast that she lives in three different worlds: The first as a wife and mother. The second is the one where "she hears the cries, the sounds of those babies abandoned in fields."[10]

"But it's the third world that I live in that makes it all possible," she says. "It is being in communion with [God] every day, being in His presence, drawing strength and love and sustenance to fight the evil that is in this world, to be His hands and feet."[11]

Kay has done some incredible work fighting and raising awareness about the terrible scourge of AIDS in Africa. But it might never have happened had she not read that timely article. It might not have happened had Kay not been primed to see that critical need.

Before we can act mercifully in a world full of need, we must see that world clearly. The ability to see that world is the first step in following the God Impulse—the first line in God's pattern of love.

But it's not easy. We have to learn to look at the world like God looks at it.

In a study about the kingdom of God I participated in, I learned that God's kingdom—sometimes called the "Upside-Down Kingdom"—was Jesus's constant paradigm. The phrase is coined by Donald Kraybill in his book of the same name.[12] Kraybill isn't talking about "the Upside Down" from Netflix's *Stranger Things*, nor is he talking about the kingdom of heaven. When we talk about God's Upside-Down Kingdom, we're talking about *our* world—but seeing it as much as we can through God's eyes: eyes that see that six is greater than seven, that less truly is more.

We don't need long to see how "seeing" is one of the biggest challenges in living that kingdom life. Indeed, in John 3:3, Jesus tells us explicitly, "Truly, truly, I say to you, unless one is born again he cannot *see* the kingdom of God" (emphasis added).

But even when one is born again, true sight can be difficult to master.

The Wool over Our Eyes

My wife and I often take our dog, Bailey, for a walk at a nearby park. It's a beautiful place filled with green trees, flowers, and a little lake. And sometimes it even has a herd of goats.

They're on the clock, these goats. A goatherd brings them in to eat the underbrush and keep the park nice and tidy. One day, while Bailey and I were passing by, I went up to the goatherd and asked him a question.

"What's the difference between sheep and goats?" I said.

The goatherd could've rattled off any number of differences. Even though the animals can look quite a bit the same, sheep and goats don't even belong to the same genus. Goats have more chromosomes than sheep (sixty to fifty-four); sheep tend to eat foliage low to the ground (like grass), while goats like their meals higher up (like leaves, shrubs, and weeds). Goats tend to be more independent too—and more ornery.[13]

But the goatherd didn't name any of those differences. Instead, he laughed. "Look at how those goats eat," he said, pointing to some of his "employees." "They eat with their heads up. They look around. They're aware of where they are and what's happening around them.

"Sheep always keep their heads down when they're eating," he went on. "I've seen a sheep get killed right next to a sheep that's eating; he won't even be fazed."

He chuckled again. "Sheep are so dumb."

There's another layer of irony in a sheep's grazing habits: sheep actually have outstanding long-range vision. Moreover, like goats, they also have excellent panoramic vision, thanks to their curious rectangular pupils, which allow for a greater range of sight. A sheep that's looking straight ahead can actually see something moving behind it, thanks to the placement of their eyes and those freaky pupils. It's almost like a superpower.

But when it comes to seeing things up close, sheep have terrible eyesight. So when sheep keep their heads down while they eat, they're actually robbing themselves of one of their greatest traits.

When it comes to sheep superpowers, they're their very own kryptonite.

In the Bible, Christians are compared more often to sheep than any other animal. Often, I think we like to see that as sort of a term of endearment. We see sheep as cute, clean creatures—fluffy and cuddly and almost petlike, under the care of a wise and understanding shepherd.

But again, that's our faulty sight talking. Shepherds know better. Sheep are dumb and are natural prey. Get close, and you'll find they're dirty and smelly too. They need a shepherd because, without one, who knows what sort of trouble they'd get into. And as we've learned, they might not even see that trouble coming. But in the eyes of the Lord, what makes the sheep more special than the goats? They so desperately need him—and they (and we) know it!

Calloused Hearts

In this chapter, we've already unpacked some dispiriting comparisons between our world and the animal world. We have shorter attention spans than the average goldfish. Like sheep, we have a tendency to "keep our heads down," focusing on ourselves and our personal matters instead of using the panoramic vision that God has blessed us with. We know that, in God's Upside-Down Kingdom, he values different things than we naturally do—and that truly seeing the world as God does requires us to reconsider our value structure entirely.

But Jesus said there's one more hurdle that causes us to stumble when it comes to seeing and feeling like God does: our own calloused hearts.

In the New International Version of the Bible, Matthew 13:15 reads: "For this people's heart has become calloused; they hardly hear with their ears, and they have closed their eyes. Otherwise they might see with their eyes, hear with their ears, understand with their hearts and turn, and I would heal them." The English Standard Version gives us a slightly different translation that still means, essentially, the same thing: "For this people's heart has grown dull, and with their ears they can barely hear, and their eyes they have closed, lest they should see with their eyes and hear with their ears and understand with their heart and turn."

In his "Exposition of the Bible," John Gill says people became "incapable of taking in the true sense and meaning of what they saw."[14] In Greek—the language that the New Testament was originally written in—the word *sklerosi* is used, meaning "hard" or "scarred." It's where we get the English word *sclerosis*, as in multiple sclerosis: it's the un-healthy hardening of body tissue.[15]

Not only do we lose the ability to see, but we lose the ability to feel.

Let me use video games as an illustration of what can happen to us.

Video games are an integral part of our entertainment landscape today. Millions of people play them. They're also exceptional training tools: studies suggest that they can improve our ability to problem solve, reflexes, hand-eye coordination, and even vision.[16] That's right: some say that gaming can help you see better.

But research also shows that violent video games can cause emotional desensitization.[17] The more we hurt and kill "people" in a virtual world, some studies suggest, the less we're able to care about suffering in the real one. Thanks to the training of video games, we can build up emotional scar tissue. We may be able to see better, technically, but our ability to feel is slowly sapped from us.

So it is with us spiritually. Sometimes we lack the ability to see and feel. But sometimes, even when we see well enough, we don't necessarily have the tenderness of heart to act on what we witness.

That's why *disposition* is so critical in this first step in God's impulse. We must be disposed to not only see but also understand what we're seeing—and when it's appropriate to act on it.

Even those of us who rarely pick up a game controller are prone to the same desensitization, aren't we? We may not "kill" enemies on-screen, but we see plenty of death and destruction on the evening news or in our Facebook feeds. In Ethiopia, we've seen children cry, their stomachs bloated and eyes covered with flies. We've seen people in Sierra Leone wail as their loved ones—victims of Ebola—are buried. We've seen the ravages of war in Mosul, the terror of Islamic militantism in Paris and Manchester.

Our world conspires to desensitize us.

"With the frequency of shootings and terror attacks there is a sense of anxiety that's building in people," psychologist

Anita Gadhia-Smith told the *New York Times* in 2016.[18] "There is a heightened alarm, but there can also be some desensitization that's happening."

It's a tragic trick of our minds: the worse the world gets, the less we're able to feel that suffering. It all seems too overwhelming. We can't get our minds around all its horrors, so we build up scar tissue. Calluses. Our hearts grow dull. We close our eyes and, when that's not possible, we close our souls.

But if desensitization is a trick of our fallen natures, there's another trick to get ourselves out of that space. And it is, quite literally, a trick.

Tricking Ourselves: Becoming More Merciful

Clearly, many things keep us from seeing and feeling the world as God wants us to. Our attention spans. Our values. Our tendency to just "look down" at our own wants and needs. Our cultural desensitization.

So what's the solution? How do we see the world as the Good Samaritan did? How do we see it as God does?

One of the tenets of making investments is the ability to trick yourself. We all know that the secret to good investing is "buying low and selling high." If you bought $1,000 worth of stock in Apple back in 1996, you just might be a millionaire now.

Of course, there was a reason why no one was buying Apple stock back in 1996. Most people thought it was a terrible, terrible idea. That year, *Time* called the company a "chaotic mess." *Fortune* said that Apple was a company investors should "probably avoid." "The idea that they're going to go back to the past to hit a big home run . . . is delusional," software developer Dave Winer told the *Financial Times* in 1997.[19] Many observers thought the company would either go belly-up or be bought by a larger, more functional business.

The only ones buying Apple stock in 1996 were either geniuses or crazy people. The "buy low, sell high" strategy seems so simple—until it comes time to slap down your money on a low-valued, high-risk investment.

Jeremy Grantham is my favorite investment expert. In 2009, during the height of the Great Recession, he wrote an article titled "Reinvesting When Terrified,"[20] advocating a disciplined reinvestment strategy even when the market's at its rock-bottom worst. It was the ultimate reminder to "buy low, sell high."

Did I act on this advice from my favorite advisor? No. I was too terrified!

"When everyone else is greedy, be afraid," goes an oft-quoted investment motto. "When everyone else is afraid, be greedy."

But here's a secret: when everyone else is afraid, chances are we're afraid too. It's human nature. So what do we do? *We have to trick ourselves.* We have to see something different from what everyone else sees. We have to imagine the possibilities that no one else can imagine. We have to see, if you will, the world upside down.

It's not easy, but it is possible. In fact, we trick ourselves all the time.

Another cliché we hear quite a bit in business is "Fake it 'til you make it." It means that, even when we don't feel confident, act confident. Not only will that confidence help give others confidence in us, but it will instill confidence in ourselves. Scientists have found that the more we smile, the happier we are. This is not because we're smiling because we're already happy; it's because smiling makes us happier.[21] When our outward attitude suggests we're happy, our inward attitude often follows suit.

Why would following the God Impulse be any different?

The Kitchen Magician

Let me confess something to you: I'm a selfish guy. I always have been. It's the natural bent in my character.

But when you get married and have small children—children who, frankly, can be pretty selfish and demanding in their own right and can't do a thing by themselves—selfishness really *does not work*. (Trust me on this. I tried.)

Lots of young parents can get pretty miserable when all the slavish devotion they gave to themselves is suddenly, and necessarily, transferred to that of a squalling, cranky kid. Moms and dads can feel resentful or depressed.

How did I escape that fate? By tricking myself.

I began calling myself the "kitchen magician." Every time I saw that the kitchen was dirty, I'd take on my new alter ego and swirl into action—scrubbing pots and pans like the superhero I imagined myself to be. I became a "poo specialist" too. Dirty diapers? *Let me at 'em!* All I was missing was a cape.

These tiresome jobs became something more: an adventure. Or so I told myself. I can't say that I ever *loved* changing dirty diapers. But I was amazed what a difference it made in my attitude. When you see yourself as the kitchen magician, suddenly you've got a reputation to uphold. You've got a countertop calling to follow.

I don't know if it's ever fun, exactly, to see and feel the hard truths of the world. But there is an element of calling in it. If we want to love the world as God does, we have to trick ourselves into seeing it as he does. We have to slip into our own alter egos—a superhero persona. We must trick ourselves into believing we are the hands and feet of God.

And the irony of that? That's exactly what we are. That's exactly who God wants us to be.

When we prayerfully try to see the world as God sees it, guess what happens? We see the world as God sees it. The Upside-Down Kingdom becomes visible to us. We begin to value the same things God values.

And our world is turned upside down in the process. We understand that, in being God's avatars on earth—seeing and feeling as he would—we, in turn, are seen and felt. We are ministered to. We see that six is greater than seven. That less is more.

Open Your Eyes

Are we about our Father's business? Are we investing in those whom God sees as important?

Jesus said, "My food is to do the will of him who sent me and to accomplish his work" (John 4:34). God's business is to *love*. But we cannot love as he does if we cannot see or feel. In the New Living Translation of that passage, the word *food* is replaced with *nourishment*.

We are not Jesus. We need to know that we are the beneficiaries of seeing and feeling. We are the ones who are nourished. We are deceived when we are like the sheep who keep our heads down and miss the panorama of God's kingdom.

It's telling, I think, that in the very next verse—John 4:35—Jesus says, "Look, I tell you, *lift up your eyes*, and see that the fields are white for harvest." Jesus is asking for us to look up. To see the harvest.

What's our new identity? Our new alter ego? It's to be "vessels of mercy," as Paul describes us in Romans 9:23. This is infinitely more consequential than being a kitchen magician or a poo specialist.

And the first step to being that vessel of mercy is relatively easy. We have to see differently. We have to look through God's eyes, feel as God feels. If we can just get the vision of being a womb for the lost, guilty, and broken, we will automatically be on the lookout to make it happen.

Lynne Hybels, wife of Bill Hybels, founding pastor of Willow Creek Community Church, has made it her business to see uncomfortable sights.

For years, Lynne's been an advocate for peace between Israel and Palestine. She's engaging in a conflict that has lasted for decades—a problem that many would say has no answer other than one side or the other giving up. But in a conflict that almost demands people take sides, Lynne refuses; instead, she sees both sides and encourages reconciliation.

"I cannot walk quietly through the halls of Yad Vashem (the Holocaust Memorial) in Jerusalem . . . without being horrified by what the Jews experienced in Europe in the 1930s and 40s," she writes in a 2011 blog post.[22] "I earnestly long for the day when Jews can live in Israel—and anywhere—in security."

But then she adds that she has seen, with her own eyes, how Palestinians are sometimes treated within Israel.

"I was shocked to see the reality of daily life under military occupation," she writes. "A shattered economy, land seizures and house demolitions, settlement expansion, Israeli-only roads networking through Palestinian land, and hundreds of military checkpoints on Palestinian roads—all these make daily life difficult and frustrating for Palestinians. Because of delays at checkpoints, produce rots in the back of pickup trucks before farmers can get it to market."[23]

At the end of another blog on the topic, Lynne quotes Mother Teresa: "If we have no peace, it is because we have forgotten that we belong to each other."[24]

Perhaps that is one of the greatest secrets of seeing and feeling mercy: that we're not so different from one another, no matter how different we may look or seem. Perhaps, if mercy were more prevalent in the Holy Land—if truth were marinated in that mercy—resolution might find itself closer to reality.

It's always a risk when we open our eyes and see. When we open our hearts and feel. But it's a bigger risk when we don't. Our eyes cloud. Our attention wanders. Our spiritual hearts can get sclerosis.

Then we can get really sick.

So, fellow sheep, I implore you: Lift up your eyes and look on the field, white for harvest. Trick yourself. Make yourself believe, in the deepest recesses of your soul, that God wants you to show his love to the world.

Because he does.

We are here to see. We are here to feel. And when we do, we will be nourished. God will restore our souls. And in the pain and struggles of the world—a hurting world we too often shut our eyes to—we will see beauty too; we will see God.

God's Pattern of Love for You: Seeing

Isn't it amazing that God gave both sheep and goats 360-degree panoramic vision when they keep their heads up? Think of an area in your life in which you have your "head down." If a person you know is involved in that area, consider reaching out to them. Ask God to open a new door in that relationship.

3

The Womb

*L*atonya Bowman, twenty-two, was nearly nine months pregnant. Though she and the unborn baby's father, ex-boyfriend Jamal Rogers, had separated some time ago, they still saw each other frequently. Indeed, in late May of 2012, the two had attended a drive-in movie together in their hometown of Detroit. After the movie, according to ABC News, they drove back to Jamal's girlfriend's house and pulled into her garage. Latonya got out of the car and was going to drive back home when she heard the garage door close unexpectedly behind her.

Suddenly someone grabbed her by the throat and pointed a gun at her head. She was forced to lie on the ground and felt duct tape wind around her hands and feet and finally cover her mouth. She was blindfolded and forced into the car.

The car roared back to life, the terrified woman cowering in the back seat as her unseen assailant twisted and turned the vehicle through Detroit's maze of streets. Finally, it crunched to a halt. She heard the driver's door open, then her own.

"You know why this is happening," Latonya's attacker said.

She didn't. She had no idea—until the man asked her just how far along her pregnancy was.

Then Latonya understood: He was going to kill her because she was pregnant. He was going to make sure that neither she nor her unborn baby would survive the night.

Suddenly, she felt liquid start to trickle over her head, her shoulders, her belly—cool, greasy, with a sweet, sharp smell. *Gasoline.*

And then she heard the strike of a match.

Whooom!

Latonya hurled herself out of the car and began to roll around on the ground frantically, trying to put the fire out. A loud crack snapped behind her. Then another as she felt a searing pain in her back. She'd been shot. Her only chance: to convince the man he'd killed her. She lay still—her whole system pulsing in pain, her body still smoking—and finally heard the man's feet pound down the alleyway, escaping what he believed was a murder scene.

But Latonya survived. She freed herself and drove to her mother's house; her mother rushed her to the hospital. A few days later, Jamal and his accomplice, Antonio Mathis, were charged with kidnapping and attempted murder—and Latonya gave birth to a perfectly healthy boy.[1]

Shaped by Love

In chapter 2, we talked about how important it is to see and feel in our fourfold pattern of love—how it's really the first step in the God Impulse. But who do we see? What do we feel? What's the point of it all?

The point of mercy, quite simply, is to take someone in need—someone who's hurting or in trouble—and bring them to a place of safety. To help them to a sheltering inn like we read in the story of the Good Samaritan. To help them feel the safe, strong arms of their heavenly Father, as we saw in chapter 1. God's impulse is all about leading people to a place of warmth and protection, a place to heal and grow stronger—be it physically, mentally, emotionally, or spiritually.

We want, in a way, to take them back to the safest place we'll ever know: the womb.

I don't use the metaphor of a womb lightly. One of the Hebrew words used for mercy is *racham*, which is related to the word *rechem*, which means "womb" in Hebrew. Both words share a common root understanding: protection from harm. "In general, in the past 6,000 years or so, the womb was the safest place for a child to be, a place where he or she would be protected from harm, which is the root of true compassion and mercy."[2] Erin Kast of the Augustine Collective notes the similarities between the two words as well. "Thus to ask for the meaning of mercy—the greatest attribute of God and one of the most cherished Christian virtues—demands the surprising question: what does it mean to be in or of the mother's womb?"[3] Philosopher Ivan Illich said that mercy is "the womb in the state of love."[4]

Obviously, pulling hidden meaning from etymology can be a dicey, uncertain proposition. But the comparisons between the protection of the womb and the protection mercy affords us are striking. "To say God is merciful means far more than to say God is compassionate or God is pitying or God is kind," writes Kast. "To say God is merciful is to say God loves us like a mother loves a child in her womb, or, rather, like the relationship of a child to the womb."[5]

We begin our lives in the womb. It's where we grow. Before we were even born, our mother's womb gave us shelter and warmth and nourishment. Ray Comfort, a New Zealand pastor and evangelist, once said that a womb should be the safest place in the world.[6] And in many ways, it is.

Look at Latonya's story again—how her attacker was determined to kill not only her but also her unborn baby. If Latonya had already given birth, the infant obviously wouldn't have stood a chance against a full-grown attacker armed with gasoline and a gun.

But protected by the mother's womb, he lived.

Think of the womb like a combination of a NASCAR roll cage and a bubblelike spaceship—only much, much more advanced. Inside are oxygen, nutrients, and warmth—everything a person needs to survive. And it's all provided seamlessly: there's no need to pack envelopes of applesauce or canisters of air; Mom supplies it all.

The baby is connected to the mother's placenta by the umbilical cord, which protects the baby's microscopic blood vessels. A mucous plug seals the womb off and protects the baby from all sorts of infections. The amniotic sac keeps germs away too, and the amniotic fluid keeps the baby cool and buffered from pressure outside. The muscles around the womb give yet more protection and insulation, while the nearby pubic bone and spinal column help protect the baby from nasty knocks and jolts.

That's what mercy's supposed to be: Warm. Safe. A harbor from the cruel, crashing sea of the world. It's like we settle into the palm of God's hand and let him carry us for a while.

Compassion, a word closely related to mercy, has an equally interesting Hebrew root: *chanan*. It means "to stoop" or "bend in kindness." To give. To bestow favor. Now, think about how many times the Bible refers to God as a merciful, compassionate God. Deuteronomy 4:31 says, "For the LORD your God is a merciful God." "Be merciful, just as your Father is merciful," Jesus said in Luke 6:36 (NIV). "The steadfast love of the LORD never ceases; his mercies never come to an end; they are new every morning; great is your faithfulness," we read in Lamentations 3:22–23. *Merciful* is, in fact, often one of the first words he uses to describe himself.

Think for a minute about how when someone asks you to describe yourself, the first words you use are telling. They indicate to your audience what you feel is most critical about who you are. They likely describe how you see yourself. And very often, you'll lead with your best attributes. "I'm a hard worker," you might say. "I care deeply about others." "I'm creative." "I'm detail-oriented." In some ways, it's like a verbal resume. "This is who I am," you're saying. "This is what's important to me."

What does God lead his resume with? How does he define himself?

I care for you. I love you. I will stoop down to serve you. I will give you a womb. He defines himself by his mercy.

The Hebrews used a different word for mercy in Deuteronomy 4:31—*hesed*—but the sense of providing a womb is still very much in play. "For the LORD your God is a merciful God," we read. "He will not leave you or destroy you or forget the covenant with your fathers that he swore to them."

Even when we're at our worst, God waits for us with open, merciful arms. "Yet even now . . . Return to the LORD your God, for he is gracious and merciful, slow to anger, and abounding in steadfast love; and he relents over disaster" (Joel 2:12–13).

Yes, of course God has far more facets to his character. He's sovereign, omnipotent (all-powerful), omniscient (all-knowing), and omnipresent (everywhere). He's slow to anger but infinitely holy and perfectly just and righteous. He's worthy of praise for all these things. But the fact that he's merciful to us when he finds us broken, addicted, and bankrupt should make us fall on our knees and worship. Then, when we need it most, he gives us warmth and safety. He cradles us and gives us space and time to recover, the opportunity to take stock of our situation and grow strong in him again.

His womb is found in the Samaritan's inn. The hug of a stranger. Food from a friend. His womb is home in the best of senses, the safe place to heal and grow, where we can be protected from the bullets and flames of the world. As Christ-followers, we need to have a vision for being that womb to others. We need to have eyes to see the systemic injustice and how it impacts the "Jamals" of the world in a totally disproportionate way. Our ability to recognize the need for individual mercy needs to grow into identifying the opportunity for societal justice too.

The Prodigal Son

One of Jesus's most famous and familiar parables is that of the prodigal son, which is recorded in Luke 15:11–32.

It's the story of a man with two sons. The younger son—a rebellious sort, you imagine as you read—walked up to his father and asked to get his inheritance early. "Father," the younger son said, "give me the share of property that is coming to me" (v. 12). And so the father did. Soon after, the younger son packed up all his newfound wealth and "took a journey into a far country, and there he squandered his property in reckless living" (v. 13).

But the good times did not last. A famine rolled through the country, forcing the prodigal son to look for work. The only job he could find was tending pigs. It must've been a terrible job, because the man was so hungry and so mistreated that he "was longing to be fed with the pods that the pigs ate, and no one gave him anything" (v. 16).

Eventually, the prodigal "came to himself" (v. 17) and remembered his father back home. He realized that his dad's servants were fed and treated far better than he was, and he decided to go back home and beg for help—for mercy, if you will. The prodigal knew he had no right to ask for much. He'd already squandered his share of the inheritance. The most he could rightfully ask for was, quite simply, a job.

Jesus explained that the son even plotted out exactly what he'd say to his father, just like we might do if we knew we were guilty of something pretty big and that someone might be really, really angry with us. "Father, I have sinned against heaven and before you," the son had planned to say to his dad. "I am no longer worthy to be called your son. Treat me as one of your hired servants" (vv. 18–19).

But when the prodigal son did come home, a curious thing happened. His father *ran* to him. Ran to him in love.

Keep in mind that a father running to greet his son was seen as shameful, even scandalous. According to theologian Matt Williams in *Biola Magazine*, "A Middle Eastern man never—never—ran."[7] To run meant hitching up your tunic and showing a bit of leg, which was not done. And to run to a son who had shamed the family name? It just wasn't done. But the prodigal's father ran anyway. Williams suggests that the father ran to protect the son from the condemnation of the community; he shamed himself to protect his son from shame.

That's mercy.

The prodigal son came home thinking he needed a job. What he really needed was mercy. A place of safety and healing. He needed the strong arms of a father, even though he didn't deserve them. He needed a *womb*.

And the father gave it to him, wrapping the son in his arms and leading him inside.

And let's remember that, in this parable, we're the prodigals. We rebel. We squander God's gifts. And then when we realize what a mess we've made of our lives, we beg for forgiveness. And our Lord, our Father, throws his arms wide and welcomes us home.

"I have exhausted every iniquity, but I have not exhausted your mercy," seventeenth-century poet and philosopher François Fénelon once said. "On the contrary, your mercy takes pleasure in overcoming my unworthiness."[8]

I love that line: "Your mercy takes pleasure in overcoming my unworthiness." When we are at our worst and most vulnerable, God is at his most merciful. The prodigal son parable paints a vivid picture of the worst you—the one where you are laid bare, all your sins are on the table, you are guilty, and yet you are loved and accepted.

If you've read my first book, you know how I came to Christ. Like the prodigal, I was far from home, both physically and spiritually. I remember walking down the street in Melbourne, Australia, totally alone and lost in my sin. I was invited to church, and I went more as a social anthropologist than a penitent sinner. I had no interest in what they "sold" there.

But when I entered that storefront gospel church, I experienced an incredible sense of love and acceptance. I felt safe. I felt cared for. I felt as though I had found a spiritual womb.

It's a wonderful, beautiful conclusion to a story, right? This moment of heartfelt reconciliation? Most of us would be satisfied if Jesus's parable ended right there.

But interestingly enough, it doesn't. It goes on.

The Older Son

When the older son heard rejoicing and revelry in his father's house, he turned to one of the servants and asked what was going on. The servant told him that his younger brother had finally come home, and their father had "killed the fattened calf, because he [had] received him back safe and sound" (Luke 15:27).

But for the older son, the prodigal's return wasn't a reason to rejoice. He was furious, in fact, and unleashed all his rage on his father.

"Look, these many years I have served you, and I never disobeyed your command," the older son told his father, "yet you never gave me a young goat, that I might celebrate with my friends. But when this"—and you can almost hear the older son spitting the words here in derision—"*son* of yours came, who has devoured your property with prostitutes, you killed the fattened calf for him!" (vv. 29–30, emphasis added).

Maybe you can understand the older brother's anger. I can. It doesn't seem fair, does it?

Jesus tells us what the father told his older son, but he doesn't detail *how* he told him. I like to imagine that he spoke with a smile, eyes crinkling at the corners, his voice full of gentleness.

"Son, you are always with me, and all that is mine is yours," the father said. But then—perhaps his eyes turning a little glassy with tears—he added, "It was fitting to celebrate and be glad, for this your brother was dead, and is alive; he was lost, and is found" (vv. 31–32).

My pastor, Randy Pope, teaches that *both* sons were lost—the younger in rebellion, the older in moralism. A moralist believes that we can somehow earn our way into God's good graces. Jesus flipped the whole construct on its head: at least the prodigal—the rebel child—repented. Rebels usually end up with the pigs, after all, where they can come to their senses. Moralists think they have nothing to repent of; they're praised for their good works and good sense. They're like the priest and the Levite in the Good Samaritan—"good" people who totally miss the point.

Christians, especially evangelical Christians, love truth. We teach truth, we preach truth, we sometimes even cram truth down other people's throats.

And truth is indeed important. But sometimes we need to see and feel mercy before we can see and feel truth.

Even when we want to tell people about the greatest truth we know—the truth that Christ came and died for our sins, that he's the way to everlasting life—showing a little mercy, kindness, and compassion can go a long way toward helping people hear that truth.

A Little Help from Far Away

India has shed its third-world status to become a global economic player. It boasts the sixth largest economy in the world, and its GDP was expected to grow by more than 7 percent during the 2017–18 fiscal year.

But visit rural India, and you'd never know it. While the big cities boom, Indian farmers have been beaten down by drought, hardship, and unscrupulous moneylenders. Many farmers have fallen into a devastating debt spiral from which it's impossible to recover. And some of these farmers, seeing no way out, find what they believe to be a permanent escape from their burdens: suicide.

Indian farmers have been killing themselves at a high rate for decades now, but the problem seems to be getting worse. According to the India International Centre, more than twelve thousand farmers have committed suicide every year since 2013.[9] "Farmers' suicide is no longer an aberration restricted to a particular region, but a nationwide pandemic," writes Raghavendra Madhu for *The Quint*.[10]

When these farmers die, they often leave more behind than just mountains of debt. They leave behind wives, sons, and daughters who are suddenly saddled with the very same problems the farmers felt they couldn't handle. That many of these farmers and their families come from India's "untouchable" caste—the lowest rung in India's age-old, discriminative, and officially outlawed social hierarchy—doesn't help.

When I heard about these farmers' widows, I knew I had to do something. It was almost as though God conditioned me to intercede. My mother was a widow, and when I was a child, I heard her cry more times than I can count. Now, after learning about these widows in India, I could hear them cry. I could see their tears.

For more than a decade, I've partnered with Din Bandhu Ministries, a Christian organization that arranges for local pastors to visit these widows and give them prayer, guidance, and sometimes more tangible help. I regularly hear about the lives that are being changed.

Take Anusaya, who lost not only her husband to suicide but also her right arm, up to the elbow. "I was helpless," she says. "I was cursing God for this life." But then Din Bandhu invited her to a program where volunteers washed her feet, gave her a rose, and embraced her (a rarity sometimes for those considered by many Indians to be literally untouchable). "I was crying when I saw the love they had and also when I heard that there is [a] God who cares for widows."

Din Bandhu also managed to provide Anusaya with four goats. And while a gift of goats might not mean much to you or me, to a rural Indian family a goat is a precious commodity, as it's a source of meat, milk, and money and an especially important safeguard amid the threat of drought. If a crop fails, a goat can put food on the table and help prevent farmers from taking out another soul-sapping loan.

Another widow, Vandana, was trying to raise two sons and a daughter when her husband became sick and died. Before he passed, the Christian farmer encouraged Vandana to set aside her Hindu idols and pray instead to Jesus. Din Bandhu helped buy Vandana a threshing machine, and she created a small "daily needs" shop. With God's help, through Din Bandhu, she was able to send her sons to college and marry off her daughter without going into debt—no small feat in a region where the bride's family is expected to provide a dowry. "I am challenging other widows to live life with dignity," she says. "Self-pity is from Satan."

Yet another woman, Mira, gave birth to *five* daughters during her marriage. Every year she and her Hindu husband would "sacrifice a goat to our goddesses," asking them to deliver a male child, who could help with the farm and provide more income. A son never came. Then, with debts mounting and no help on the horizon, Mira's husband killed himself. The suicide left Mira without income, without a home, without hope. She admits that she considered killing herself too. But then she encountered Din Bandhu, which came alongside her and provided money for medicine and to cover the cost of some of her daughters' educations.

"[I came] to know the Lord who will never leave me," she says. "I believed in Jesus, and I'm alive today because of him. Today we do not worship goddesses, but we know [the] true loving and living God."

Goats. Threshing machines. Medicine. Like the Good Samaritan, Din Bandhu came alongside these women, picked them up, and helped them with some of their most urgent material needs. But it went beyond that too. Din Bandhu provided these widows with a *womb*. That womb—that mercy shown in times of critical need—allowed them to heal. To grow. To find God, the author of all love and mercy. Since I've been involved in this program, more than six hundred widows have become Christians. I think these women were receptive to the truth of the gospel because of the mercy shown to them.

As a Christian, I believe in the Great Commission: "Go and make disciples of all nations, baptizing them in the name of the Father and of the Son and of the Holy Spirit, and teaching them to obey everything I have commanded you" (Matt. 28:19–20 NIV).

But his teachings and truth don't always mean much to people who are hurting and heartbroken. Jesus's feeding of the five thousand feels hollow when we've got hunger pangs in our own stomachs.

We need mercy. It's the bridge that takes us from our brokenness to God's glorious truth. It's the womb that allows us to heal and grow so we can see and feel Jesus's saving work more clearly and powerfully.

But there's another remarkable aspect of mercy: It doesn't just impact the person who receives it. It changes the person who gives it.

Mercy's Ripple Effect

We all know that a baby is shaped by the mother's womb. But I find it profound that the mother is also shaped by the baby.

Seems strange, doesn't it? But it's absolutely true, as science makes clear. Pregnancy supercharges the mother's production of hormones, such as progesterone and estrogen. In fact, a woman will generate more estrogen during *one pregnancy* than throughout the rest of her nonpregnant life.[11] Her breasts enlarge. Her posture changes. Often expectant mothers will experience alterations in hair growth. And while many women experience a change or diminishing of taste while pregnant, sometimes their other senses—particularly their sense of smell—grow more acute. We could go on, of course. Every anatomical system in the mother's body is impacted by her pregnancy.

That includes the brain, by the way. A recent study found that pregnancy can change the size and structure of brain regions dedicated to thoughts, feelings, and beliefs—and those changes can last for at least *two years*.[12]

Obviously, providing a merciful, metaphorical womb doesn't induce the same radical changes on us physically. But mentally? Emotionally? Spiritually? When we see and show mercy, it changes us. Shapes us. Transforms us. Through the process of mercy—following God's impulse—we become, step-by-step, a little more like the person God wants us to be.

And you know what? Science backs that up too.

Reams of studies suggest we become healthier, happier people when we show compassion and kindness to those around us. Some even point to a "happiness effect" when we volunteer.[13]

When we help others, our bodies release endorphins—natural chemicals that make us feel good.[14] Volunteers and do-gooders report feeling more grateful and more satisfied. These feelings are so pronounced that scientists have even coined a term for it: a "helper's high." Do a Google search for the term, and you'll need to sift through more than three hundred thousand results.

According to scientists at the London School of Economics, volunteers typically report being significantly happier than those who don't. Indeed, the more we volunteer, the statistically happier we're likely to be. People who volunteered for a favorite charity every month were, on average, 7 percent more likely to say they were "very happy." Those who volunteered every week were 16 percent more likely to be "very happy." Amazing, isn't it?[15]

And even though our bodies don't go through quite the physiological changes of a pregnant mother, there's evidence that showing kindness and compassion can even help us physically as well. People who volunteer report experiencing fewer nagging pains.[16] Volunteers fifty-five and older tend to live longer. Dr. Christine Carter says in *Psychology Today* that "volunteering is nearly as beneficial to our health as quitting smoking!"[17]

Giving mercy and showing compassion feels good. Why do you think that is? Could it be that God designed us that way? That he wants us to feel joy when we're mirroring one of his most critical attributes?

We don't always just feel joy when we show mercy, of course. Mercy can be hard, really hard, and we'll get into that later in this book.

But I've felt the joy of giving mercy firsthand.

I've looked into the eyes of Indian widows. I've held their rough, work-worn hands in mine. I've prayed with them. And it felt like the tables had flipped: I wasn't ministering to them; they were ministering to me.

God's Treasure House

We've already talked about how mercy is a critical part of God's character. We know that it's also a gift from him—the greatest gift imaginable.

But God does more than show us his mercy. He explicitly commands us to imitate him in this way—to show mercy to others just as he's shown mercy to us. Take a look at what

Jesus says in Luke 6:36: "Be merciful, just as your Father is merciful" (NIV). It doesn't get more explicit than that.

It's also interesting that Jesus tells us to imitate the Father in this passage. Remember, Jesus is really considered our prime role model on earth. Peter, Paul, even Jesus himself repeatedly say throughout Scripture to imitate Christ, as he is the exact representation of God (see Heb. 1:3). But here Christ himself implores us to imitate his Father. Why? Because the Father showed mercy on us from practically the very beginning. The moment we broke the world, God began showering us with his forgiveness and embracing us with his womb, and he's been doing it ever since. Consider Ephesians 2:4–5, where God clearly initiates the process of mercy, using his Son as a catalyst:

> But because of his great love for us, God, who is rich in mercy, made us alive with Christ even when we were dead in transgressions. (NIV)

We see God's character so clearly here—and we see an element of that character that resonates with me as a businessman. This verse describes how God views his own wealth.

Look at that verse again: "rich in mercy," it says.

In the business world, if someone's successful, we'll typically know how they made their money. We'll say, "She's a tech executive," for instance. Or "He made his money in trucking." Oftentimes we'll gauge the wealth and success of someone based on how they *spend* their money. We look at Jay Leno's garage of hundreds of classic cars or Johnny Depp's private island or the Queen of England's unparalleled art collection. How someone spends their money shows us what they value.

God, we know, created everything. He owns everything. How can we gauge his wealth? How do we know what he values? This verse says it all. *Rich in mercy*. God's very nature is love; he has a vast storehouse of mercy to spend on his creation.

Psalms 103 and 145 emphasize God's abundance of love and mercy. In Lamentations 3:23, we're told that his mercies are "new every morning." When God remakes the stone tablets for Moses and his people in Exodus 34 (after Moses broke the first set in fury at his "stiff-necked" Hebrew followers), it's an example of showing mercy.

We read in Exodus 34:6, "The LORD, the LORD, the compassionate and gracious God, slow to anger, abounding in love and faithfulness" (NIV).

And then, in the Beatitudes, Jesus invites us in on the action.

"Blessed are the merciful, for they shall receive mercy," Jesus said (Matt. 5:7). This cycle of God not only dispenses ultimate mercy on the cross but also gives us more mercy when we show that same mercy.

In effect, God is saying, "You build a bridge for someone, and I will bridge you." Or "You construct a womb to protect others, and I will be a womb for you."

And this is where our adventures in mercy really begin!

A Deal You Shouldn't Refuse

Let's go back to Ephesians 2:4–5 again. It tells us that God is *rich* in mercy. And he spent that mercy on *us*, dipping his hand into his boundless storehouse. God is love.

And then, after we've received his mercy, he asks us to spread some of it. He asks us to join him.

Let that sink in for a minute. You and I—flawed, broken people with nothing to offer the Author of creation—are being called to join him in a sacred, holy, and incredibly important job. God wants you and me to see the need for mercy in this fallen world of ours and feel his own impulse to reach out and do the work he's already done for us.

He wants us to help heal the world. In effect, he's inviting us to become his business partner.

It's hard to imagine, isn't it? God asking *us* for help? But that's what's happening.

For years, I worked with a powerful business partner—a European billionaire who gave me a great deal of latitude to invest his capital and oversee the businesses I had bought for him. I was his avatar, in a sense. I represented him and his interests.

At first, I was quite cautious with his resources. As our relationship grew, I began to find more confidence—not in myself, but in him. We began to play tennis and racquetball together, to laugh and tell stories. I started taking greater and greater risks, knowing he was with me and for me.

This attitude allowed me to think of God—who is so much more loving and forgiving than my partner was—in a fuller way. I began to lose my fear, and I took much greater risks in his kingdom both financially and relationally.

When we know we've got a powerful backer in our corner, we take more chances and riskier chances. We're given a greater ability to succeed. We discover our best opportunity to soar.

How much more daring would we be if we knew we were partnering with the Creator of the cosmos? Just how much more success could we experience if he were to give us a key to his treasure house? His storehouse of mercy?

We're called into partnership with God. We're called to be his avatars on earth—his hands, feet, voice, and heart. He's got our backs. He's given us a blank check. He's signed our marching orders to go show mercy in a merciless world. We would be crazy not to take advantage of the opportunity.

We rarely think about our relationship with God as a business deal. But when we give to the poor, we're partnering with God. We're serving as his representatives on earth. And here's the thing. God tells us explicitly that he'll repay us. Indeed, we can recoup the merciful investments we make a hundred-fold.

It seems like a no-brainer, right? God promises us so much. The need is so great. We should be diving into this grand adventure of mercy with a cry of joy. We should be clamoring to build bridges. We should be gleeful to shape wombs.

And yet so often, we're not. We hold back.

Why?

Maybe it's because we doubt God and his promises. Or maybe we tell ourselves we lack time. We can't spare the effort. We're hurting ourselves; we don't have the energy to heal the hurts of others.

But sometimes it's because we're scared to death. "What if they hurt me?" we tell ourselves. "What if they cheat me? What if they want more than I'm willing to give? What if they *need* more?"

Mercy, when done right, is terrifying. It's risky. It's messy. We don't slide it into a half-hour slot in our weekly calendar. We don't squeeze it in like a morning run or an afternoon coffee. Like a womb, it can be all-encompassing.

And who has time for that?

92

I wonder whether we don't want our lives upended by mercy. Sure, we want to change people's lives, but we don't want to be changed ourselves. We like our houses and creature comforts, Netflix after work and football on Sundays.

What is a womb? A place of warmth and safety. But what does it mean to fill that womb? We've already said it: it means changing your life. Not just for a little while, but perhaps forever.

The Price of Mercy

We've already talked about some of the physiological and psychological changes that can occur during pregnancy, but any mother can tell you it goes far, far deeper.

Expectant moms change their diets and drinking habits. They eat for two. They endure morning sickness and sleepless nights and wildly fluctuating moods for their unborn child. They deal with terrible pain during childbirth.

And then, when the baby is finally born—when it takes its first breath, opens its mouth, and begins to wail—the realization hits that the work is just beginning. Priorities reset. Life will never—ever—be the same.

Committing to God's vision of mercy—embracing God's own critical impulse—is a little like that. When we show mercy, we're committing to caring not just for ourselves, but for someone else. And when we genuinely care for someone, our commitment has few limits.

To make a commitment like that requires more than a sound, sober devotion to a business partnership, even with God. It requires more than promises of recompense. It demands more than a general desire to do good in the world.

It demands our heart.

In 2002, I began a charitable group called Geronimo, named after the Native American hero. It is said that Geronimo had a vision that he would never be killed in battle. So whenever he got into an actual battle, he would ride his horse to where the fighting was most intense. I love this! The idea behind Geronimo was to come alongside the church and show mercy—daring, risky, God-like mercy—to the six categories of people mentioned in Matthew 25: the hungry, the thirsty, the naked, the sick, prisoners, and strangers. I wanted it to be a catalyst for real change. When I approached people, I would ask them two questions:

1. Do you think the poor and distressed will be more important than we think when we get to heaven? (Everyone said yes to this.)

2. What type of eternal investment portfolio do you have that could bless the six groups of people Jesus identified with? (It seems like it is a "final exam" of sorts with our Savior. Almost no one had a plan or strategy.)

During the three years of the program, about fifty people came alongside the initiative, funding projects in twenty-six different countries. It wasn't easy for my partners and me to choose which worthy initiatives to support. So we asked ourselves one critical question.

What makes you cry?

Using that criterion, we helped hundreds of physically disabled children achieve greater mobility. We sent young Native American leaders to college. We rescued more than one hundred girls locked in forced prostitution. We freed five hundred others from modern-day slavery. We tried to "ride" to the toughest battles and be a blessing.

On one trip to India, I met one woman who'd spent much of her life working enslaved in a rock quarry, her hands sometimes in shackles. She was not alone. Her whole family was enslaved. They all worked using hand mallets to pry minerals from the hard, hot ground. They'd been threatened. Beaten. When two men escaped from one such quarry, two other slaves were punished in their stead. Every day the men would work under supervision; every night they would be beaten with a yellow rope and thrown into a small, cement room.[18]

The International Justice Mission, with an assist from Geronimo, eventually found out about one of these quarries and informed the Indian authorities. In response, India turned the quarry's operation over to the workers themselves. Many continue to do the hot, grueling work that the quarry demands, but there's a difference: they can come and go freely now. They earn a living wage. Mercy made it possible.

But is it really that much of a difference?

I asked the woman that very question—how she felt about the quarry then, and how she feels about it now.

The woman didn't say a word. Instead, she picked up a rock from the quarry—one representing her work now—and held it close to her heart. Then, to represent the quarry from before, she picked up another rock. She spit on it, threw it to the ground, and kicked it.

And then she hugged me.

I still have a pair of handcuffs once worn by one of those former slaves—a slave who now is free.

What makes me cry? That makes me cry.

As a postscript, Geronimo shut down because of a lack of interest and support. In the three years, we met many faithful Christians—many who gave to their churches, family ministries, missionaries, their kids' schools, and church building programs. Also, it seemed so many had taken on a tremendous amount of debt that blocked them from greater generosity. It seemed that the "least" were getting the "least." Review the sidebar on page 98 that details the incredible promises of blessing to those who are kind to and bless the vulnerable. It touches the heart of God when we open ourselves to being a womb.

Born Again

Our embrace of the Lord needs to be a passionate one. And when we choose to imitate God's own impulse, that too needs to be passionate.

When the Pharisees asked Jesus what the greatest commandment was, he said, "Love the Lord your God with all your heart and with all your soul and with all your mind" (Matt. 22:37). I find it interesting that mind is listed third.

Mercy is frightening, and it should be. Mercy goes beyond the bounds of good business and good sense. When we show mercy—real mercy as God intended—it carries with it the threat to sweep us away. To do crazy things in its name. To go beyond the bounds of our church-approved ideas of charity and kindness and literally change lives—including our own.

Mercy is a manifestation of love. And love is the most frustrating, most frightening, most glorious, and most powerful force in the universe. It is not rational. It is not logical. Love is a whirlwind. A tumbling, roaring ocean. A sunrise. A mountain. A magnolia. A mother's unbound, breathtaking devotion to her child.

The God Impulse is all that and more. It is connected to the riches of God's mercy. It is connected to the passion God has for his creation. The passion he has for us.

Mercy isn't always fair. We can't help everyone. But we can help *someone*.

Mercy is a womb. In its folds something beautiful can happen. Something incredible can grow. It nurtures us, protects us, feeds us, saves us. It changes us.

And when we embrace the womb of mercy, we can all be born. Born again.

God's Pattern of Love for You: Feeling

Meditate on the quote "Your mercy takes pleasure in overcoming my unworthiness." If you feel insecure or unworthy in an area today, know that God is pleased to extend his mercy to you. Satan, however, wants you to be stuck in this place of insecurity. So ask God to show you his mercy today. Also ask him to show you one person to whom you can be a bridge.

The Rewards of Mercy

When God asks us to go into business with him in this pattern of love, he wants us to feel his own impulse inside of us. But he also promises a litany of blessings too—our reward for working with him.

And you know what? He put the deal in writing.

Take a look at what God promises in the following verses if we care for and show mercy to others:

Blessing of life. "If a man. . . . gives his bread to the hungry and covers the naked with a garment . . . he shall surely live" (Ezek. 18:5, 16–17).

Blessing of family. "His descendants will be mighty on earth. . . . he has given freely to the poor" (Ps. 112:2, 9 NASB).

Blessing of met needs. "He who gives to the poor will never want" (Prov. 28:27 NASB).

Blessing of health. "How blessed is he who considers the helpless. . . . The LORD will sustain him upon his sickbed; in his illness, You restore him to health" (Ps. 41:1, 3 NASB).

Blessing of guidance and prayers answered. "Divide your bread with the hungry and bring the homeless poor into the house; when you see the naked, to cover him; and not to hide yourself from your own flesh[.] Then your light will break out like the dawn, and your recovery will speedily spring forth; and your righteousness will go before you; the glory of the LORD will be your rear guard. Then you will call, and the LORD will answer; you will cry, and He will say, 'Here I am.' . . . Give yourself to the hungry and satisfy the desire of the afflicted, then your light will rise in darkness and your gloom will become like midday. And the LORD will continually guide you, and satisfy your desire in scorched places, and give strength to your bones; and you will be like a watered garden, and like a spring of water whose waters do not fail" (Isa. 58:7–11 NASB).

Blessing of delivery and protection. "How blessed is he who considers the helpless; the LORD will deliver him in a day of trouble. The LORD will protect him and keep him alive" (Ps. 41:1–2 NASB).

Blessing of honor. "He has given freely to the poor, . . . his horn will be exalted in honor" (Ps. 112:9 NASB).

Blessing of rewarding work. "You shall generously give to [the poor], and your heart shall not be grieved when you give to him, because for this thing the LORD your God will bless you in all your work and in all your undertakings" (Deut. 15:10 NASB).

Blessing of wealth. "Whoever is generous to the poor lends to the LORD, and He will repay him for his deed" (Prov. 19:17).

Blessing of spiritual fruitfulness. "And let our people learn to devote themselves to good works, so as to help cases of urgent need, and not be unfruitful" (Titus 3:14).

Blessing of happiness. "Happy is he who is gracious to the poor" (Prov. 14:21 NASB).

Moreover, God promises one final blessing on us when we show mercy: he promises that we'll know him better—maybe the greatest blessing of all. "He pled the cause of the afflicted and needy. . . . Is not that what it means to know Me?" (Jer. 22:16 NASB).

God promises us that we'll know him better through mercy. Because when we practice one of God's most telling attributes, how could we not?

PART 2

GO:
The Discovery of Mercy

GO AND BE RECONCILED

[The Samaritan] went to him. (Luke 10:34)

4

The Last Hour

From the time he was six years old, Welles Crowther wore a red bandanna.

His father gave it to him, explaining the clean white handkerchief in his breast pocket was "for show," the red bandanna was "for blow." The white one should look nice. The red one was for the dirty work of life.

Welles took that red bandanna everywhere. When he volunteered with the Empire Hook and Ladder Company at age sixteen—joining his father on the force—he carried it with him. When he played lacrosse for Boston College, he tied it around his head and wore it under his helmet. Even when he took a job as an equities trader, working on the 104th floor of the World Trade Center's South Tower, he brought it with him. In a culture of starched white handkerchiefs folded neatly in Italian-suit breast pockets, Welles kept his bandanna close.

And it was with him on September 11, 2001, when United Airlines Flight 175—a burly Boeing 767 carrying sixty-five people—exploded into the South Tower, cutting a fatal swath between floors 78 and 85.

Several floors below Welles, Lin Yung was blown back by the explosion. When she recovered her senses, Lin still couldn't see anything at first—her eyeglasses were covered in blood. When she wiped them off, Lin saw a world of nightmare: mangled bodies strewn around her, dust and debris everywhere. She knew she was lucky she hadn't been killed right away—but she felt that even if she took a step, the tower might crumble beneath her. Lin didn't know how long her luck would hold.[1]

Then she saw a young man through the smoke and ash, seemingly more shadow than flesh.

"I found the stairs," he said. "Follow me."

Welles led Lin and others down seventeen flights of stairs, from floor 78 to floor 61, where firefighters led survivors down another twenty floors to a set of still-working elevators.

But Welles didn't follow them. Instead, he went back up, a red bandanna wrapped around his nose and mouth.

He found Judy Wein in the rubble—her arm was broken, ribs cracked. One of her lungs was punctured. Welles came in and started literally putting out fires. Then he called out: "Everyone who can stand, stand now. If you can help others, do so."

Welles led Judy down the stairs, again to a band of waiting firefighters.

And then he went back up. Again.

Welles didn't make it out of the South Tower. Perhaps he never expected to. His body was found six months later, surrounded by the bodies of uniformed firefighters. It's said that he saved perhaps as many as a dozen people that day.

He was twenty-four years old.

"People can live 100 years and not have the compassion, the wherewithal to do what he did," Wein told CNN.[2]

Lin keeps a photo of Welles in her apartment. "Without him, I wouldn't be here," she says. "He saved my life. And he will always be in my heart. Always be with me."[3]

Welles is gone, but his bandanna is not. It's part of the 9/11 museum now, and it's become a symbol of the man's heroism and self-sacrifice.[4] Snowboarder Tyler Jewell, one of Welles's old lacrosse teammates, wore a red bandanna when he competed in the 2006 Winter Olympics. Boston College sponsors the Welles Remy Crowther Red Bandanna 5K every October, honoring his legacy. ESPN writer Tom Rinaldi published a book in 2016 on Welles's legacy. Its title? *The Red Bandanna*, of course.[5]

Think mercy can't change the world? Take a look at Welles Crowther. Take a look at the people he saved. Think again.

The Secret Truths

"If you can help others, do so," Welles said. God is saying the same thing to us every day. Every minute.

In chapters 2 and 3, we began to unpack what it means to follow God's impulse—to show mercy to a world that desperately needs it. But it's not enough to *see* and *feel* the need. We must *go*. That's the second step in this four-step pattern of love. To show God's mercy, we must plunge into that need, just as Welles plunged upward—into the doomed building again and again.

Not all of us will face the same threats to life and limb, obviously. But make no mistake: mercy always carries an element of risk, even danger. To get involved—to sink your hands into the muck of the world and pull out the poor and suffering—is never safe.

But how can we ever understand mercy in the same way that Welles Crowther did? After all, it's one thing to read about the Good Samaritan in the Bible—a fictional story that Jesus told to make a point. We can all see ourselves going, as the Samaritan did, to help the injured traveler. We know how the story ends—with the visitor well cared for and the Samaritan going on his way, promising to return.

But Welles Crowther? We know how his story ends too. Would we have had that sort of courage in the same situation? What inspires someone to ignore all common sense, to risk their life and dive into such an apocalyptic scene again and again?

Three elements—three truths, if you will—were key to Welles's actions. And they can be key to ours as well.

1. First, Welles had a sense of identity.

Welles knew who he was. That identity was summed up in that red bandanna—a link between him and his firefighting father, Jefferson Crowther. In an ESPN video, Jefferson says that he and Welles were best friends. Jefferson even has the number 19—Welles's old lacrosse number—tattooed over his heart.

In the video, Jefferson quotes the Bible: "Greater love hath no man than this, that a man lay down his life for his friends."[6] Welles knew that verse—John 15:13. He embraced the values of his family. He knew who he was and what he wanted to do with his life. Indeed, shortly before 9/11, Welles called up his father and admitted he was thinking about changing careers: he wanted to be a firefighter.

That bandanna tied Welles to his father, and to the up-bringing and legacy his dad represented.

2. Next, Welles was committed to giving his first and best.

This is almost a foreign concept today, the idea of giving up our first and best to God and others. Often, we feed our scraps to charity, like we'd feed our dinner leftovers to the dog. But that's not what God wants us to do.

Throughout the Old Testament, God repeatedly told his people to bring him their firstfruits and best animals for sacrifice. He scolded those who don't do so: "When you offer blind animals in sacrifice, is that not evil? And when you offer those that are lame or sick, is that not evil? Present that to your governor; will he accept you or show you favor?" (Mal. 1:8).

Clearly, giving our first and best to God—or to those who clearly need God's mercy—wasn't any easier back then than it is now. But I think it's absolutely critical to give our first and best. In fact, it's one of my life's missions to encourage people to give of themselves not just generously but sacrificially.

In 2013, I founded The Reimagine Group, which is an organization that has worked with more than one thousand churches to encourage holistic generosity. We tell people God doesn't want their giving to stop at the offering plate. He wants us to give all of ourselves. We've learned one very important truth: *if we are not giving our first and best to God, we will not give our first and best to one another.*

But very often we keep the first and the best for ourselves, and if we give anything at all, it's often what we don't need or want. It's our garage-sale gifts, our last and our worst.

In our multiweek "Living Generosity" film and study series, we call such gifts "stinky sheep." They're not our first sheep. They're not our best sheep. They're the blind and lame and ugly ones that, frankly, we just want out of our pens. And when we give our stinky sheep to God, we're likely to be pretty tightfisted with our friends and neighbors too.

But the reverse is also true: God knows that if we give our best to him, it's *easy* to give our best to our neighbor. For example, Pastor Glen was in the midst of the "Living Generosity" series when a neighbor approached him and asked to borrow Glen's weed trimmer. "Sure," Glen said, and he pulled out a dilapidated, beaten-up Weed eater bought several administrations ago. Then he went to the store and bought himself a shiny new weed trimmer.

But it wasn't long before Glen began to wonder whether he'd been guilty of withholding his "good sheep" for himself and giving his "stinky sheep" to his neighbor. So Glen went back to the place he purchased his new trimmer and bought a second one—this one for his neighbor.

Here's another example: Matt was involved in the same "Living Generosity" series when he noticed that his church's worship leader was playing a cheap, frazzled, bargain-basement guitar during service. Matt knows a bad guitar when he sees one, mind you. He *collects* guitars, some of which are ludicrously valuable. His favorite? A classic Martin acoustic guitar—the same brand of guitar played by everyone from Elvis Presley and Woody Guthrie to John Lennon and Johnny Cash. The most expensive Martin ever sold belonged to legendary guitarist Eric Clapton. The 1939 model he used to play "Tears in Heaven" on MTV was auctioned off for $791,500.

I don't know if Matt's guitar had a similar pedigree. But I do know that, of all the guitars that hung on his wall, the Martin was Matt's favorite. His best sheep.

Matt took down that Martin, drove it to church, and gave it to the worship leader.

"For where your treasure is, there your heart will be also," reads Matthew 6:21. Our hearts follow our treasure. When we see someone spending their treasure on sports cars or fine food or lavish vacations, we have a pretty good idea about what they prioritize. Sometimes such things even become our idols. When we give our good sheep to those priorities and give our stinky sheep to God, we know where our hearts are. But when we give God our treasure, our hearts will be with him.

The heart of worship is seeing the connection between worship and sacrifice. In fact, we worship God *through* our sacrifice.

It's easy to forget that today, when our church services label "worship time" as the time when we all sing together. Nothing wrong with singing, of course, but it leads to a mis understanding. *Worship is music*, we think, *and the offering is money*. But the truth is, our offerings are worship too. It's not only about how we demonstrate our love for God, but how we demonstrate that love—where our priorities lie—for ourselves and one another. God asks us to give our first and best to him. When we do so (or when we don't), the focus of our hearts becomes very clear.

But as I've said, giving isn't all about money. It's about our time too. Our skills. Our attention. Our emotion. And perhaps most importantly, it's the hope and capacity that get built into the lives of the recipients of mercy. And as in

Welles's case, sometimes giving encompasses our very lives. To take the second step on the path of mercy—to "go" as God asks us to—can be an open-ended directive. And we never necessarily know where it might lead.

3. Lastly, loving leads to giving, which leads to going.

Running through the middle of that fiery South Tower, Welles probably wasn't thinking about whether he "loved" the people he was saving. Maybe he was operating on instinct. Maybe he was remembering his father and what would make him proud. Maybe he was thinking about God—and about what God would want him to do. We can't say for sure what was going through his mind.

But maybe it doesn't matter. Because whatever he was thinking, his motivation was rooted, unquestionably and undeniably, in *love*. Be it love for God, love for his father, love for his fellow men and women, or all three. When the world around him was literally falling apart, Welles found clarity in following God's impulse. And that impulse is rooted, always, in love.

But in our own lives, even when we give like God wants us to, we don't always love in the midst of our giving, do we? Sometimes we give not only sparingly but also grudgingly.

It's easy for this to happen. It can feel inevitable. We're faced with a dizzying number of needs, and they multiply like rabbits. If we always waited until we felt like giving—until we felt God's impulse at work in our hearts—how many needs would never get met? Sacrificing ourselves, our time and treasure, can seem like the antithesis of what we actually want to do.

And yet when our hearts are aligned with God's, we *will* want to do it. Not because it's fun, but because we know

110

that's what God is all about, and we want to be all about that too.

We all know that loving can be hard. Love can hurt. It's not always fun. Loving a child who's disappointed you again and again, or loving a father who scarred you deeply, isn't always easy.

And the same can be said when we give through love. It can be painful.

Frankly, it should be painful sometimes. But that doesn't take away the beauty of giving and going. Rather, it augments it.

In John 3:16, God shows us that he "so loved the world" that he gave up the thing most precious to him—his only Son. First John 3:16 points to how we should follow his example: "By this we know love, that he laid down his life for us, and we ought to lay down our lives for the brothers."

These two verses highlight that love precedes giving. This is the issue I have with various generosity initiatives; they try to bifurcate love and giving and often ignore the relational component entirely.

I have a saying: "Relationships create context; money never does." If a stranger were to plop ten thousand dollars in front of you and walk out of the room, you'd be dumbfounded. You'd ask yourself, *Is it a loan? A gift? Proceeds from an illicit drug sale?* Because you don't have a relationship with the giver, you have no context for the gift. First Corinthians 13:3 says, "If I give away all I have, and if I deliver up my body to be burned, but have not love, I gain nothing." God wants you to pray, to really see and feel, and if he leads, to *go*. Obviously, there are fine charities where the relational component is simply not possible. The point is, too much

111

is 501(c)(3) and (4) giving and a failure to bridge people personally.

Not too long ago, a man came up to me to chat for a bit after a talk I gave. Now, this man was very wealthy. But when he looked at me, I could see pain in his eyes.

"I've given away more than fifty million dollars," he admitted to me. "And none of it was with love."

Staggering.

We all know that fifty million dollars can cure a lot of ills. I know his gifts funded some good work. I know they made a difference.

But to follow God's impulse—to see a hurt in the world and go salve it—is about more than writing checks, no matter how many zeroes they have attached to the end of them. To go in God's mercy is to follow his impulse. To risk for the good of others. To feel. To love.

Once we understand the Father's love, we'll want to give of ourselves and of our resources. When we get to this point, we simply go where God tells us to go.

But be warned: in doing so, we must be prepared for the unexpected.

Building Some Unexpected Bridges

I've already talked a bit about the work I support in India—helping widows and orphans in the most desperate of straits and freeing modern slaves from their bondage. One day, a former partner of mine who originally came from India told me he was organizing a fund-raiser for Geronimo and inviting a group of about forty to fifty business leaders from across Atlanta.

Naturally, I was flattered and grateful. I arrived at the restaurant and the room was filled with Indian doctors, lawyers, and professionals. Many of them stood to talk and they all donated financially to the cause. "Thank you," one man said. "We love our country and often get too busy to think about how we can help. When we heard of all the different initiatives that Geronimo was funding, we wanted to come alongside you and help."

We were able to present the heart of God for people in their country. It was humbling. Virtually all the people at the fund-raiser were Hindus, but the work of mercy for the oppressed and poor united us and built an unexpected bridge.

When we follow this pattern of love and enter into this world of mercy, we may sometimes be surprised how God uses us. And when we go in mercy, sometimes we're surprised by what we're led to do. We give away our prized guitars. We buy neighbors weed trimmers. Sometimes we even run into burning buildings.

But sometimes, when we *are* prepared to go, God stops us. This happened multiple times in Jesus's and Paul's ministries. For example, in Acts 16:6, it says that Paul and his companions traveled to two regions "having been kept by the Holy Spirit from preaching the word in the province of Asia" (NIV). We need to listen when God says stop.

Going On (and Taking Off-Ramps)

Imagine for a minute that we've felt God's impulse. That we've seen an area—a place, a person, an issue—that's in desperate need of mercy. We've felt the need. Now, we're ready to go.

But don't go just yet.

Remember, this step in the pattern of love is all about discovery. It's about going, but going prayerfully and with our eyes wide open. We have to see and feel the need for mercy, but unlike those sheep in chapter 2, we must be mindful of our environment. Before we take this step, we need to recognize where our foot might land.

Sometimes God's pattern of love just makes sense to follow—a win-win for everyone involved. Sometimes it's difficult to follow, requiring time and effort and sacrifice—but we still feel God's hand on us to take that step.

But the truth is, we're not always called to show mercy. Remember what Paul wrote in Romans 9:15? "I will have mercy on whom I have mercy, and I will have compassion on whom I have compassion" (NIV). That means that sometimes God *didn't* show mercy.

Jesus didn't heal every person or address every need. According to Mark 14:7, "The poor you will always have with you" (NIV). Even the Son of God himself could not, at that time, be a salve for every hurt or sorrow. And we can't be either. We need to be mindful of that somber truth in our own merciful journey. We need to think through a situation before jumping in with both feet.

When I get to the second step in following the God Impulse—going onward into mercy—I fall back on my business instincts.

In business, even after I make a handshake deal with someone, both the other person and I must do extensive research before we complete the deal and draw up the paperwork. We do our due diligence. Do the numbers back up our initial assumptions? Does this partnership still make sense for both of us? Are there areas of concern that might require a bit more time to work through? Yes, every time I invest in a business, there's an element of risk. But that risk is mitigated by research, trends, and a bevy of other considerations. A risk? Of course—but an educated one.

Mercy is, as we've said, inherently risky too—much more so than business. We don't go into an act of mercy with the promise of profit or dividends. We're "investing" in someone or something for *their* sake, not ours. And we always have to be mindful that, in following God's impulse, showing mercy doesn't always make sense to us.

But sometimes showing mercy doesn't always make sense for God either—and he has ways of telling us so. Even as we live a life of mercy, God gives us what I call "off-ramps" along the way. We have the opportunity, and sometimes the responsibility, to stop and back up. Here are some examples of how God can communicate to us that we might not need to pursue a certain situation.

1. Mercy is counterproductive.

I love the saying "Always be merciful until you get to the point that granting further mercy would not be merciful." Remember that while mercy is a prime facet of God's character, so is justice. And sometimes the most merciful thing we can do is stand aside and let God reveal his pure, virtuous side.

Several years ago, I mentored a young man who'd spent time in jail for shooting someone in the kneecap. I had known him for years. He'd spent time on some of the roughest streets in Atlanta and grown up without a father in a deeply problematic home. He asked that I go to court with him as a character witness, which I did. Due to the severity of what he had done, he had to go to prison.

When the man got out of prison, I hired him. More than that, we would meet together every week to pray and go through some goals together. I felt really good about the decision. He bought new clothes and it seemed as though he had a new life too.

Then he borrowed money from some fellow employees and was caught selling and taking drugs and was sent back to prison. It broke my heart.

We can show mercy to the hurting all we want, but those hurting people have to be in a place where they can receive it too. This young man wasn't. In this case, and in many others, justice is a kind of mercy too.

2. When you're counseled against it.

Before you dive into a risky, merciful situation, it's always a good idea to talk with people you trust about that situation. Discuss it with your spouse. Talk it over with some godly friends. Bring it up to your parents. If they warn you about getting involved, it's important to prayerfully consider their opinions and, in all likelihood, follow them.

3. Be mindful of your own safety and the safety of your family.

Again, mercy's inherently risky. Sometimes following mercy can require a great deal of sacrifice—even, as we saw in the first part of this chapter, the ultimate sacrifice. But we need to be careful not to offer that level of sacrifice unwisely. In most cases, mercy requires only our time and talents, not our very lives. And we need to be mindful of protecting both ourselves and those closest to us from what are sometimes our own best intentions.

4. Watch out for codependence.

Say you pay someone's rent for a month. Then another month. Then another. Perhaps that sort of help is needed. But when such a relationship goes on for too long, you'd be wise to begin asking yourself whether you're giving that someone a critical helping hand or providing him a crutch—even though he's more than capable of walking by himself.

Doing something for someone else, even with the best intentions, can create an unhealthy dependency, and that subverts what mercy's all about. Remember, mercy provides a womb—not a permanent place of residence. When you think that a merciful relationship is becoming a dependent relationship, you need to take an off-ramp, for both your sake and their sake.

5. Listen to the Holy Spirit.

We should always seek the Holy Spirit's guidance and confirm what we think are his promptings. It can be difficult. There is no formula, after all. Sometimes we'll be called to take risks. Other times—as counterintuitive as this may sound—we'll be called to not be involved.

As we stand on the edge of going into mercy, we can be guided by one simple question: What is their story? When we really see someone—when we take the time and effort to get to know them and their situation—we can better feel

God's prompting. We can be more sensitive to his guidance, and feel him potentially leading us to go into mercy . . . or not. And that leads us to the primary purpose of mercy: reconciliation.

Our Motive and Our Purpose: Reconciliation

It might not seem that mercy and reconciliation are invariably tied together. After all, what does feeding a hungry orphan or giving a job to a widow have to do with reconciling? It's not like you need to patch up your relationship with them. It's not like they need to make restitution with you.

But when you dive into Scripture, you see the two elements are more intertwined than you might think. Look at 2 Corinthians 5:18–20:

> All this is from God, who through Christ reconciled us to himself and gave us the ministry of reconciliation; that is, in Christ God was reconciling the world to himself, not counting their trespasses against them, and entrusting to us the message of reconciliation. Therefore, we are ambassadors for Christ, God making his appeal through us. We implore you on behalf of Christ, be reconciled to God.

We just looked at a bunch of reasons why we might not go into mercy—why God might call us to take an off-ramp. But as we weigh whether to go forward or exit, all our decisions need to be viewed through this lens of reconciliation. See, mercy is a helping hand in a fallen world. Society's sin and brokenness give rise to pain, suffering, and injustice—all the terrible symptoms of a people who've broken with God and his design for us.

If you go into a merciful endeavor, will it further the reconciliation process? Will it bring someone closer to God?

The verse above tells us that Christ literally appointed each and every one of his followers to be an ambassador in this broken world. Our jobs, schools, neighborhoods, and friendships are, at times, like foreign lands—places we go as God's agents to represent him. Our mercy is our gift, a gesture from our holy Sender. We are making this "appeal" on his behalf. He has done the work of "making peace through his blood, shed on the cross" (Col. 1:20 NIV).

When we show mercy, we're demonstrating to the world that there's a better way. Looking for help? Hope? Peace? You can find it in God, we say. And through our feeble efforts, we illustrate—to a very small degree—what God's mercy looks like. We're trying to show them that moment of ultimate reconciliation between God and us: the cross.

But there's more connecting mercy and reconciliation than just our being ambassadors on God's behalf. It's for us too.

Truth is, we can never truly forgive others if we don't have a heart of mercy. In showing mercy to a stranger, we learn how to be merciful to an enemy—or even a friend or relative who hurt us. And let's not forget that, in the Lord's Prayer, Jesus connects our willingness to forgive *others* to God's willingness to forgive *us*.

During his address to Venture Christian Church in Silicon Valley in 2017, Bishop Claude Alexander addressed the topic of racial reconciliation—an issue that touches on much of what we've talked about in the last few paragraphs. After fairly and beautifully summarizing many of the laws and practices that have oppressed and discriminated against black Americans for hundreds of years, Alexander asked those in the congregation to turn to one another and say, "It is not your fault. But it is your problem."

We're not at fault for slavery or Jim Crow laws or the racial policies of the past. But it is our responsibility to do what we can to rectify our ancestors' mistakes.

Look at our world—broken, dirty, disappointing. Most of it is not our fault. But we do bear a responsibility to go, to be ambassadors, and when God leads us, to take risks and show mercy to a world that really needs it.

Our Responsibility and Our Identity

God is a sending God. When Isaiah was asked, "Whom shall I send? And who will go for us?" he replied, "Here am I. Send me!" (Isa. 6:8 NIV). This doesn't mean we must all be missionaries. But it does mean we need to hear, see, and have open hearts to build relationships and go in an internal sense. Right after this exchange with Isaiah, God said, "'Be ever hearing, but never understanding; be ever seeing, but never perceiving' . . . the heart of this people [is] calloused" (vv. 9–10 NIV).

But the real shift occurs when we move from responsibility to identity. Welles's identity was set with a red bandanna when he was just six years old. In just about every story you read about the 9/11 hero, that bandanna is mentioned as a "link between father and son."

I love that.

Our heavenly Father has given us a similar link: a bloody red cross. At the foot of that cross is where we should find our identity. And God chose one word to motivate his people to become sacrifices for others: *mercies*. In Romans 12:1,

Paul writes, "By the mercies of God . . . present your bodies as a living sacrifice, holy and acceptable to God, which is your spiritual worship." Sacrifice is our identity and our responsibility.

The Jews so hated the Samaritans that they destroyed the Samaritans' place of worship on Mount Gerizim. They would not even travel through Samaria. But Jesus used a Samaritan as the protagonist for one of his most poignant parables. And as my friend and theologian Walter Brueggemann says, it changed the Samaritan's identity. For over two thousand years, he has been called "good."

Just as we get reshaped when we become a womb for others, seeing ourselves as ones who go can change our identities from just Thomas to Good Thomas. Good Charlotte. Even Good Jack.

God's Pattern of Love for You: Going

Going is an adventure. We always discover something new. In business, going to a customer's office always changes our perspective. It makes us ask questions, such as what are their needs? How can I serve them?

Do you have a neighbor you have not talked to recently? Has someone in your sphere experienced a loss or a sickness in their family? These are small but significant ways that we can go.

The Innkeeper's Take

We've talked a lot about most of the people in the Good Samaritan story: the victimized traveler, the priest and the Levite, and the Samaritan himself.

Not many think much about the innkeeper. But as a man who's worked for years in the travel industry, I often wonder what he thought of the whole thing. What would this fictional innkeeper say if he were interviewed?

"We get all kinds here," he might say, sitting outside the inn. He'd point to the road. "They call it 'the Bloody Way.' Some say it's because of the color of the rocks, but those of us who know this area know different."

He'd lean in closer, lowering his voice. "The blood spilt here gave the Bloody Way its name. The bandits, the vagabonds—this pass is *dangerous*. I've seen more than my share of death on this corner. More than my share of misery. Sometimes it seems I run a clinic here as much as an inn.

"But lucky for me, travelers take the risk," he would say with a sigh. "For all the danger, there's no shorter road from Jerusalem to Jericho, and people these days are always in a hurry. Like I said, I see all kinds. Jericho's booming now—a hotbed of Roman activity. Merchants take the road, selling wares at one place, then the other. Priests take the road too, going from tabernacle to tabernacle. And, of course, people travel to Jericho for the holiday."

And then the innkeeper would smile. "But the Samaritan," he'd say, shaking his upward-pointed finger in emphasis, "the Samaritan was special. He traveled the road regularly, from Bethel to Gerizim, I believe he said. The inn is right on the way, so he'd stop by often.

"That injured traveler . . ." the innkeeper would say with a shake of his head. "Well, don't like to think about it much. His condition, that is. Bad business. Didn't think he was going to make it for a while.

"But it wasn't the first time the Samaritan showed care for complete strangers—strangers who, if they simply met on the streets, would probably avoid the Samaritan like a leper! He's paid for dinner for travelers before—widows with dirty kids in tow, too poor to pay for a room. Oh, he's paid for their lodgings too.

"You'd think he'd stop. True, the man seems wealthy enough. Each time I see him, his donkey's loaded with wine or oil or other goods. He's an exception. The richer folks are, the less willing they are to spend it, I say." Again, he'd smile. "But not the Samaritan. It's like he's got a . . . a secret of some kind. For all the money he gives away, he's about the happiest person I see come by.

"In fact," he says, leaning in, "I *like* to see him. And I don't like many." He would pause, leaning back against the wall. "Something special about him. It's like—I know this sounds crazy. He's a Samaritan, after all. But it's almost like he's good with God.

"Imagine," he'd say, casting his eyes upward toward the desert-blue sky. "A Good Samaritan."

5

A Price Paid

THINKING MERCY FOR FELLOW SINNERS

*M*y chief financial officer walked into my office holding a handful of papers. He frowned—never a good sign. He slapped the papers on my desk.

"Take a look," he said. "We were right."

I felt my stomach clench. I picked up the papers—expense reports—and began to leaf through them one by one, already knowing what they said. The numbers told a painful, deceitful story: Tom was cheating. An extra meal here. A forged receipt there. The fraudulent expense reports went on for months.

Tom had taken from the company—the company he helped create and I now managed—thousands of dollars.

I wasn't blindsided. I knew this was a possibility. But I still felt like I'd been punched in the gut.

Tom was a promising go-getter—a tall guy with a charismatic smile, a Texas drawl, and a steely business sense. He was a natural leader with boundless potential. But Tom hadn't really found his niche yet. To me, he felt a little aimless, a little uncertain. Now the numbers confirmed my worst fears about him. He and a couple of his associates had decided to use the company—*our* company—as their own personal ATM machine. They were stealing from us and undercutting our business's future.

"Thou shalt not steal," the Bible says. The law doesn't get much clearer. Exodus says if you steal an ox and sell it, you owe the guy another five. Steal a car today, and you could go to jail. Steal from a company? It warrants at least termination, maybe worse. After all, to steal from your own company is an act of betrayal—to its shareholders, its employees, and the company itself. That's serious stuff. In Dante Alighieri's epic poem *Inferno*, traitors land in the ninth circle of hell.

I thanked my financial officer, watched him leave, and then shut my door. I bowed my head and began to pray. "How should I handle this, Lord?" I asked. "What should I do?"

I weighed the matter for a couple of days. And as I deliberated, I thought of Proverbs 19:11: "Good sense makes one slow to anger, and it is his glory to overlook an offense."

Glory? I thought. *Is it glorious to overlook what Tom did to us? To our company?* I didn't want to overlook this offense. He deserved punishment.

Glory in Hebrew means beauty, bravery, and honor. Is it honorable to overlook someone who's cheating? Someone who's stealing? It didn't seem fair.

I kept thinking. I kept praying. And then, a few days later, I called Tom into my office.

He came in, looking uncharacteristically nervous. I asked him to shut the door. He did and sat down, his hands clasped in front of him, pale and jittery.

"Tom," I said. "As you know, we've just purchased a few companies down in Alabama, and we'll need someone to head that division and tie them together—someone who could go down there and really unite them. Make them part of our team."

I paused. "Is that something you'd be interested in doing for us?"

His eyes grew wide. A small smile curled on his face. Tom didn't need to think about it long; he accepted the opportunity in the space of a heartbeat.

But I wasn't done with him.

"Now, you know what that means, Tom," I said, my voice growing stern. "We need you to represent us well. I'll come and visit you every month and see that you have all the support you need, and we'll be watching everything—*everything*—you do."

That was the closest I came to giving him a reprimand. I never mentioned those expense reports. Never told him that I knew he'd been cheating. I don't know if he ever suspected that I did.

But I do know this: Tom never cheated the company again. The division he headed did extremely well, becoming one of the company's highest performing. He stayed with us for another eight years, and during that time Tom was one of our most valuable assets.

Not a Reward

When we talk about the second step in this pattern of love, we are exploring and must have a measure of caution in how we go into mercy. We must be thoughtful. We should consider carefully whether God's calling us to show his mercy in any given situation. Sometimes we receive a hard answer: it's best not to go. We take an off-ramp.

But other times, we feel God whisper to us to enter into that second step of mercy, even when our own voice tells us to hold back. It may not make sense at first. And yet we feel the nudge of the Holy Spirit pushing us into uncomfortable situations for the eventual betterment of us all.

Mercy is often about giving one a place of safety—a warm, protected retreat. But while the merciful recipient feels safe, the merciful giver is often anything but. For them—for us, if we're following God's impulse—mercy is daring. It is always costly.

Honestly, many who need our mercy the most are people who might not seem to deserve it. Or so we think. As Tim Keller writes in his book *Ministries of Mercy*, many of us divide the poor and needy into two categories: (1) the deserving, whose need is not their fault, and (2) the undeserving, whose need is caused by their own sin and foolishness.[1]

But Keller points out that everyone deserves our compassion. "Our aid is called mercy, not a reward," he says.[2] I like that.

Price Paid

In chapter 3, I said that one of the Hebrew words for mercy was related to the word for *womb*, but the Latin variation of mercy means something quite different: a price paid.

For Christians, there's obviously a deep spiritual resonance with that phrase. Look in the Bible and those words—or the significance behind them—are everywhere. Take Galatians 3:14, for example: "Christ paid the price so that the blessing promised to Abraham would come to all the people of the world through Jesus Christ and we would receive the promised Spirit through faith" (GW).

But the original sense of the word was a bit more pragmatic. Literally in Latin, the word *merces* means "wage" or "reward." It comes from the ancient world of bottom-line transactions, seemingly wholly removed from that metaphorical sense of warmth and safety we saw in chapter 1.

As you might expect, *merces* resonates with a businessman like me.

But as Latin spread and slowly changed into a bevy of Romance languages, the word itself seemed to take on richer and deeper meaning. *Merces* became *merci* in French, meaning "thank you" or gratitude for a service rendered. It became *mercê* in Portuguese, *merced* in Spanish, *mercede* in Italian—all of which mean essentially what the English word *mercy* means today.

The word has moved a long way from that Latin sense of a "wage" or "reward" *earned*. It's about something *given*, and given freely. When you throw yourself on "the mercy of the court," you're not claiming innocence; you're not offering to bribe the judge. You're admitting guilt but hoping the court will somehow see fit to reduce or waive the sentence—to pay, in essence, a portion of your debt to society. When a ship is at the "mercy of the waves," the phrase itself suggests that it comes into that watery world as an interloper, a debtor. The ship is on borrowed time, but perhaps it can get an extension.

Mercy still implies a transaction. But it's a transaction in which one side seems to have all the power and all the control—and carries the transaction's entire burden. There's no earthly obligation to show mercy. There's no contract that spells out how someone must respond to that mercy. Every time mercy is extended, the books of justice do not balance. A price is paid—and the "wrong" person or party is the one who pays it.

Think of the mercy extended to each of us in Christ. Proverbs tells us that it's not wise to take responsibility for the debts of others. But Jesus did just that when he took our sins, and the penalty for them, upon his own body; he suffered incredibly and died.

Many people I know have a buttoned-down faith built on truth, justice, and "the American way." It sounds more like Superman than a biblical faith. When we begin dispensing mercy to sinners and enemies, listen for the howls. "Justice is not being done!"

But what makes it complicated is that with this type of mercy, there is always a calculation.

Once, when I was working with my billionaire owner and partner, I purchased a smaller competitor of the company I ran. Some of the assets of the other company were deemed "too risky," so four of us bought those assets in our own names rather than under the company. We ended up making a modest profit on the transaction and afterward a wave of guilt came over me. *So they were too risky for the company but not too risky for me?* I tried to soothe my conscience by telling myself that it wasn't very much money.

I decided I needed to talk with my billionaire partner and offer to turn the funds over to the company. He could've been mad. He could've asked for the profit. Instead, he sat back with a big grin on his face. He looked at me and said, "Jack, thank you for telling me. I would not have wanted to hear it from someone else. It's no problem." And he let me keep the small profit I had made.

Why is it that we always seem to want mercy for ourselves and justice for everyone else?

When we receive mercy, it motivates us to extend mercy to others. Because this billionaire showed me mercy that day, my loyalty to him was reinforced. It also illustrated for me both the need to show mercy to others and the benefits of doing so. On the surface, it seems that mercy is not a smart business practice, but it can be. We always need to think and pray, but God gives us an interesting promise in the Beatitudes: "Blessed are the merciful, for they shall receive mercy" (Matt. 5:7).

Showing mercy can pay off in even more intrinsic, tangible ways too. That second step of mercy—going into a person's mess and pain and difficulty to help and heal—can seem, at first glance, completely illogical and feel utterly foolish. But God's foolishness outstrips human wisdom, and you may come to find that showing mercy just makes *sense*.

Weighing Options

The God Impulse is, on some level, about balancing mercy and truth—giving people what they *need* while being conscious of what they *deserve*. In the story at the beginning of the chapter, Tom didn't get what he deserved; he got mercy along with an opportunity. Grace usually follows mercy. And it turned out to be just what Tom needed. That act of mercy benefited not only him but also our entire operation.

Every parent has felt the difficulty of achieving that balance with their children. What do you do when your kid scrawls his name all over the kitchen cabinets in orange crayon? Brings home a D in reading? Disobeys you? Talks back to Grandma?

Do I exact discipline or do I show mercy? you ask yourself.

Sometimes the answer is easy. Other times, not so much. You want your children to follow your rules and expectations. But sometimes circumstances get in the way. Sometimes we have to consider extenuating circumstances. Was that D in reading a result of laziness? Or was your child struggling? Was that rude outburst a sign that your daughter's fighting with her friends? Do you need to send her to a time-out? Have a long heart-to-heart with her? Both?

Sometimes, even when children do something very, obviously wrong, a gentler hand is required. Justice may be warranted, but you know that showing mercy will bring greater dividends.

When we ignore mercy as parents, we can fail our children. Even when we follow the letter of whatever law we've set down for our kids, we can miss the spirit of it entirely. We can fail them.

Let me give you another example—a sort of prodigal son story in reverse.

When a friend of mine was a young man, he left home for college—something many people do. While he was there he fell in love. Again, nothing too unusual.

But then this young man got his girlfriend pregnant, and suddenly it felt as though the world was falling apart.

The young man—we'll call him Ben—came from a deeply religious family. He'd been trained from his earliest days to love God and hold his commandments precious.

He wasn't a prodigal. In fact, he was like the "other" son, the one who stayed home, operated the ranch, and carried out all his father's orders to the letter. But like the prodigal, perhaps, Ben had big dreams—dreams of seeing the world before settling down. And now, with just two simple words— "I'm pregnant"—everything changed.

Neither Ben nor his girlfriend considered abortion. She wouldn't give the child up for adoption either, and Ben couldn't imagine leaving the love of his life in the lurch. So he fashioned an engagement ring out of a twist tie, got down on one knee, and proposed. He blinked back tears, saying goodbye to the life he had hoped for and hello to an uncertain, dangerous future.

And then came the next step—the one he'd been dreading more than any other: Ben picked up the phone and dialed home.

Imagine, for a moment, being Ben's parents. They get a call—unexpected but welcome. He was a grown man, of course. But in a way, he was still their little boy. When Ben was young, his mother would read to him every night—Dr. Seuss and *Winnie-the-Pooh*, *Just So Stories*, and the Chronicles of Narnia. They gave him piano lessons and took him to baseball practice. They encouraged every interest and praised every victory. As a family, they went to church every Sunday and prayed every night. For twenty years, they'd invested all they had in Ben—time, talent, and treasure—and sent him off to college where every indication was that he'd find success and happiness.

And then they heard this: "She's pregnant."

It was as if he'd taken the phone receiver and smashed a lifetime's worth of dreams they had for him.

Can you blame Ben's mom for crying? Can you blame Ben's dad for what he said next?

"I'm so disappointed in you," he said.

The receiver went dead. Ben, even with his fiancée beside him and a new life growing unseen, had never felt so alone.

Do I discipline or do I hug?

You could argue that Ben deserved the "discipline" he got that afternoon. He deserved his parents' tears, their anger, their disappointment. He had disappointed them. He had turned his back on what sort of man they'd raised him to be.

But in that moment, Ben didn't need to be told that he had broken their hearts. He knew it already.

He needed a womb. He needed his father's strong arms—even if he only felt them through the phone.

Ben's father didn't give him that safe place, a place of warmth and comfort and unconditional love. He couldn't. The hug wasn't possible.

I believe Ben's dad failed Ben in that moment. Today, more than twenty-five years after the fact, Ben still tears up when he talks about it. What if he had said, "I love you, Ben. From the time you were born, I have been so proud to call you my son. You know this is not news I wanted to hear, but we as a family are behind you and will give this new little child all the love and support we can."

Each of us is given a handful of critical moments in our relationships—moments when we desperately need mercy, and maybe more importantly, moments when we desperately need to *show* mercy. Those moments are not always easy to see, and sometimes they can be impossible to act on. But if we can show mercy in those critical moments, we can make a universe of difference. The God Impulse sets us up for love, forgiveness, and grace. Vengeance and punishment are usually best left to God. Appropriate discipline is another matter.

We Don't Always Feel Merciful

Do I discipline or do I hug?

It's easy to be merciful to those we think deserve it. Those poor widows in India, for instance. Orphans begging for handouts. The beaten traveler in the Good Samaritan story. When it comes to the feeling side of mercy, we do feel the God Impulse.

But what happens when we don't feel like being merciful? When those who need that mercy have hurt or betrayed us? The Toms in our lives? The Bens? The first step in the pattern of love is to *see* and *feel* the need for mercy. But what happens when you don't feel like being merciful at all?

The feeling side of mercy is easy for me. But sometimes mercy isn't the outflowing of our natural inclinations—a real God Impulse in our lives. Sometimes it's hard. We have to make a conscious choice to show mercy. And we don't always choose well.

When we show mercy to others, we're acting, in a way, like parents would. And just like parents, we Christians can have a particularly hard time figuring out how to balance God's boundless mercy and his unflagging thirst for truth and righteousness. Honestly, I think we have difficulty seeing how God himself even does it. In fact, in my research, plenty of fine theologians suggest that mercy—at least as far as God's concerned—is done. He's given all the mercy he's going to give.

Naturally, these theologians point to the work done on the cross, and rightly so. "There it is," they say. "The ultimate act of mercy. Christ paid the price." Boom.

But they see it as a one-time transaction. Because of Christ's boundless sacrifice, the need for daily doses of mercy is behind us.

135

"The truth is God does not show mercy without punishing sin," writes pastor and author John MacArthur. "For him to offer mercy without punishment would negate his justice."[3] He then quotes Dr. Donald Grey Barnhouse, who wrote in his study on Romans, "When Jesus Christ died on the cross, all the work of God for man's salvation passed out of the realm of prophecy and became historical fact. God has now had mercy upon us."[4]

That's all totally on target. God gave us his mercy in that act on the cross. It's the climactic example of what outrageous, scandalous mercy looks like. But then Barnhouse goes on to write: "For anyone to pray 'God have mercy on me,' is the equivalent of asking him to repeat the sacrifice of Christ."[5]

Now, mercy is a complex concept, no question. And Barnhouse and MacArthur—both of whom have far more theological training than I do—are absolutely right that God's ultimate act of mercy saved us. All our sins—past, present, and future—were carried up to that cross and paid for through Christ's blood. But I would ask them, "How can we be a witness of God's mercy to the lost whom we want to lead to Christ?"

I think about Ben, the young man we just talked about.

Ben was a Christian when he got his girlfriend pregnant. His salvation wasn't in question here. But did he need a little mercy? You bet. And he believes he got it—eventually.

Perhaps MacArthur's spiritual dynamics were in play with Ben, who believed, in the days after his girlfriend got pregnant, that God was *punishing* him. He had sex before marriage—the pregnancy was his comeuppance. It was the punishment that, he believed, would keep on punishing—earning him the shame and scorn of those closest to him.

But then, a few days later, his parents came alongside him and offered the support he so desperately needed. And when the baby was born, Ben and his girlfriend—now his wife—were surrounded by friends and family. They helped feed and wash the child. They babysat while Ben and his wife studied for final exams.

And the help didn't end with graduation. His photo albums are filled with beautiful holidays and happy memories.

It wasn't always easy, but being part of a family never is. But ask Ben if he would've wanted his life to go any other way, and he'll say no.

A punishment? Perhaps. But a blessing too.

Such is the strange, beautiful calculus of God's merciful transactions. As J. R. R. Tolkien supposedly once wrote to a fan, "A divine 'punishment' is also a divine 'gift,' if accepted."

Ben didn't just receive love from his friends and family; he received mercy from his merciful God. And it wasn't just the mercy on the cross; it was mercy *renewed daily*. Mercy that met him right where he was.

Yes, our sins were forgiven that day Jesus hung on the cross more than two thousand years ago. I believe in that act of mercy. But I believe we could still use God's mercy *every* day—and more often than not, we get it. Jesus says in the Beatitudes, "Blessed are the merciful, for they shall receive mercy" (Matt. 5:7). This suggests to me that we continue to receive mercy as we show mercy. Mercy isn't a onetime deal. We're replenished by it all the time, as a lake is replenished by the rivers and streams that flow into it. We need what the King James Bible calls God's "tender mercies"—plural, you'll note—every morning.

Mercy is more than an action. Mercy, for God and for us, is an attitude—an attitude that God reveals to us constantly and asks that we follow; it's an impulse we should heed whenever we can.

Even when sometimes we don't want to.

Pardon Me?

When I gave Tom his promotion despite his cheating the company, it wasn't just because I felt God wanted me to. It seemed like the right thing to do.

Tom had tons of talent, but he hung out with other employees who, I knew, were less than honorable in their dealings with the company. Promoting Tom and moving him to Alabama achieved three things. First, it separated him from those associates. Second, his new duties allowed him to use his talents more fully and effectively; he liked his job more and, as such, grew more loyal to the company. And third, the nature of the job forced him to be more accountable. Yes, I believe promoting Tom was an act of mercy, but it was also sound business.

Alexander Hamilton—a founding father and a brilliant financial and political strategist—understood how a little well-placed mercy could help oil the mechanizations of government. In 1788, he penned what's now known as the Federalist Paper 74, outlining the need for the power of pardons.

In seasons of insurrection or rebellion, there are often critical moments, when a well-timed offer of pardon to the insurgents or rebels may restore the tranquility of the commonwealth; and which if suffered to pass unimproved, it may never be possible to recover after all. It was reasoned that some crises could be allayed or overcome if the belligerents could be given a deal forgiving them for their trespasses.[6]

Let me repeat the crux of the paper: Hamilton argued that a "well-timed" offer of pardon could defuse a combustible situation.

Just six years later, President George Washington was faced with just such a combustible situation—the Whiskey Rebellion. Farmers in western Pennsylvania were angry about a tax on whiskey—the first tax on a domestic good in young America's history. They refused to pay, attacked tax collectors, and eventually, marched on the home of a prominent tax inspector and set it on fire. Washington himself led an army against the rebels, capturing about 150 of them and prompting the rest to disband.[7]

Two men were convicted of high treason—for which the punishment was hanging. But Washington pardoned them instead. Washington's strong-armed response to the rebellion itself, and his clemency for individuals swept up in it, helped the young nation survive its first internal crisis and set a pattern for presidents to come. He used both justice and mercy to preserve a country.

Since then, all but two presidents have used their power to pardon (the two who didn't—William Henry Harrison and James Garfield—died very early in their first terms).[8] John Adams, Andrew Johnson, and Jimmy Carter, among others, have used their power to restore or forgive soldiers who deserted or dodged the draft. Franklin Delano Roosevelt pardoned nearly 3,700 people during his three-plus terms in office, the most of any president.[9] (Unless we count Andrew Johnson's Christmas Day pardoning of every Confederate soldier in 1868.)[10] Abraham Lincoln was famous for his clemency—so much so that his generals complained that he used his pardoning power too much.

"If a man had more than one life, I think a little hanging would not hurt this one," Lincoln once said. "But after he is once dead we cannot bring him back, no matter how sorry we may be."[11]

Once he is dead we cannot bring him back. Did you know that 159 prisoners on death row have been pardoned, acquitted, or had charges dismissed against them when new evidence was found?[12] Even more significantly, according to the Death Penalty Information Center, some states might've killed men who were innocent of the crimes of which they were convicted.[13] There's no way to determine how many innocent people might've been accidentally executed; few crimes are investigated after the supposed culprit is dead.

Sometimes mercy isn't only the right thing to do; it's the smart, prudent thing to do—even when we don't want to do it. And sometimes when we withhold that mercy, we do everyone, including ourselves, a disservice.

When to use mercy is not an easy question for anyone, much less a president. On his last day in office in 2017, President Barack Obama used his presidential pardoning power to commute the sentence of Chelsea Manning, who was convicted of stealing 750,000 secret government documents and giving them to WikiLeaks.[14] He commuted the sentences of a number of crack, heroin, and methamphetamine dealers as well.

But Obama withheld clemency from thousands of others serving life sentences for relatively minor drug-related offenses. Both John Knock and Michael Pelletier, despite massive campaigns pleading for clemency for them, were not on Obama's final list in 2017. Pelletier's case was particularly notable, given the fact that he's been paralyzed since childhood. His crime—possession and distribution of marijuana—was relatively minor, and a petition for his release garnered more than one hundred thousand signatures.[15]

"If a paraplegic serving life for pot is not worthy, then who is?" said Amy Ralston Povah, founder of the CAN-DO foundation, an organization that pushes for mercy for many convicted criminals and whose slogan is "Justice through clemency."[16]

Some would argue that such criminals don't deserve pardons. They don't deserve mercy. They committed a crime. They were fairly convicted. They deserve the punishment.

But do they? Does everyone in prison deserve to be there? Could there be extenuating circumstances we just don't know about?

Seeing Clearly

Look around almost any courthouse in the Western world, and you'll likely see a statue of Lady Justice. She typically holds a scale or balance in one hand and a sword in the other. And most tellingly, she's blindfolded.

The blindfold is meant to indicate her impartiality. She'll mete out justice to those who come before her, regardless of how rich or powerful or charismatic they might be.

Justice is blind. And it should be.

But mercy—mercy *sees*. As we witnessed with the Samaritan, it sees and feels, goes, does, and endures for the poor, the distressed, fellow sinners, and enemies.

It sees the extenuating circumstances behind the crime. It sees the pain of the families involved. It sees what good might come from clemency. It dares to hope that compassion and forgiveness can lead to healing—and can eventually benefit not only the pardoned but also the pardoner and society itself.

The truth is, social inequity and racial bias haunt our society. Some people are dealt a bad hand from the very beginning. They grow up in neighborhoods surrounded by drug dealers. Their families are decimated by poverty and bad decisions. Maybe they learn the hard rules of the streets from their older brothers and sisters. Maybe they're pushed over to the wrong side of the law by their own parents.

Yes, everybody has the freedom to make their own choices, and maybe they have an obligation to make good ones. But the choices I've had to make are very different from what someone who grew up in the slums of Detroit or Boston might've been faced with. I've never had to choose between shoplifting groceries or going hungry. I've never had to choose whether to obey my mother and break the law, or obey the law and hurt my mother.

When we decide to go into mercy, we have to ask an important question: What's their story? What circumstances pushed them into an unwinnable situation? What baggage do they carry that makes it hard for them to make good choices?

When we're willing to listen to someone's story, it's easier to go into mercy—to follow God's impulse even when it's hard.

In 2003, Republican Illinois governor George Ryan pardoned four death-row inmates three days before his term ended. Though the inmates had confessed to their crimes, they later insisted those confessions had been extracted under torture by Commander Jon Burge, who was later fired from the police force.[17]

In his decision, Ryan referenced another story of Abraham Lincoln, who gave a soldier a pardon even though there was no outcry to do so.

"I shall be his friend," Lincoln allegedly said.

"Today, I shall be a friend to [these four inmates]," Ryan said. "Today, I am pardoning them of the crimes for which these four men were wrongly prosecuted and sentenced to die."

The next day, Ryan went a step further—commuting the death sentences of 167 inmates on death row. "Our capital system is haunted by the demon of error—error in determining guilt, and error in determining who among the guilty deserves to die," he said. "What effect was race having? What effect was poverty having?"[18]

Some were outraged by Ryan's actions, naturally.

"Every one of the victims, he has killed them all over again," said Cathy Drobney, whose daughter was murdered by one of Illinois's death-row inmates.[19]

But since then, Ryan has also been repeatedly nominated for the Nobel Peace Prize—even as he served his own term in prison for corruption.

The Calculus of Mercy

Was Ryan right to commute those death-penalty sentences? Right to pardon the four convicted murderers? We may differ on those issues. We might have done things differently.

But he heard their stories. He understood there was more to their convictions than met the eye. And it moved him to mercy.

There's no question that just as our society wrestles with mercy, so must we. We must ask the difficult questions of when to hug and when to discipline. And as much as I think we should try to always err in favor of mercy, that doesn't mean it's the right answer all the time. God's character, however, appears to be bent toward it. Micah 6:8 says to "act justly and love mercy" (NIV). James 2:13 says that "mercy triumphs over judgment." To follow God's impulse—to replicate his merciful character—doesn't mean we should check our brains at the door. As we saw in the last chapter, we have to be smart about it and be aware that sometimes we come to a spot where mercy just isn't viable anymore.

We also have to understand that mercy, in some instances, can come with its own set of strings. Commuting a sentence only lessens the punishment; it doesn't wipe away the record of the crime. A reprieve postpones sentencing. A whole gamut of legal actions express mercy without completely erasing the slate. Likewise, just because we show someone mercy doesn't mean the person is freed from all obligations or excused from compensation. Sometimes those factors remain in play.

And remember that, in certain cases, justice *is* mercy. We can show mercy in telling someone how grievously they hurt us. We can even show mercy in sending someone to jail (which, for some, can be itself a sort of womb). People who commit habitual sins or crimes *must* be corrected. We should still forgive someone in our heart, but that doesn't mean we must protect them from all the ramifications of their own sin and wrongdoing.

To see just how difficult the calculus of mercy can be, we need look no further than the immigration debate raging in our country.

It's true that millions of people are here illegally—more than eleven million, in fact, according to the Pew Research Center.[20] By definition, these men and women are breaking the law. We are a nation of laws. And there's no question what the law says we should do: deport them.

Blind justice.

But what are their stories?

When we look at the issue through the eye of mercy, we see the stories. We see the families that could conceivably be broken apart by strict adherence to the law. Marriages could be destroyed. Children could be torn away from parents.

And then we have to consider that many of these laws being broken haven't actually been enforced for decades, which makes the law and the government itself complicit in this outcome. It's as if the government is a lax parent, setting a curfew for her teen but never enforcing it—until years later when she decides at random to ground the kid for breaking curfew. That's bad parenting, we'd say.

And we also must remember that the Bible tells us explicitly to treat strangers and aliens kindly. "Do not neglect to show hospitality to strangers, for thereby some have entertained angels unawares" (Heb. 13:2). "Do no wrong or violence to the resident alien, the fatherless, and the widow, nor shed innocent blood in this place" (Jer. 22:3). Leviticus 19:10 tells us to leave food "for the poor and for the sojourner."

God asks us to look at foreigners—at immigrants, legal or not—with a merciful eye.

When it comes to this issue, we need to look for a merciful compromise. Truth is important. Justice is critical. But it always needs to be marinated in mercy to be most effective.

The Price of Forgiveness

Merces. Price paid.

God paid the price for us through the death of his Son on the cross. Through Jesus, he forgave our sins. It's the clearest, most beautiful illustration of boundless mercy imaginable.

Because of that act of mercy, we Christians can think that we're off the hook. "We can't make our way to heaven through works," we say. "We're saved in spite of our sins." And that's true.

But.

Just because we live under God's mercy doesn't mean we're free from all expectations.

Those of us in America live in what we consider a "free" country—and we are free. But we still have certain *duties* to uphold. We're required to serve on a jury if asked. We pay taxes. They're just part of the deal—what we, as Americans, are expected to do.

God's kingdom is a little like that. We have certain duties that God expects of us, and a primary duty is to forgive others, just as we were forgiven.

Want proof? Consider the most famous prayer in all of Christendom, the Lord's Prayer, taught by Jesus himself.

We know it by heart, right? When we recite it at church, the words roll off our tongue: "And forgive us our debts/As we forgive our debtors." Other churches have it as "Forgive us our trespasses/As we forgive those who trespass against us."

For many people, the meaning is simple: we should forgive people just as God forgave us. God's mercy comes first; our mercy comes after.

But when you look at the original Scripture, that's not exactly what the prayer says. Jesus actually said, "For if you forgive others their trespasses, *your heavenly Father will also forgive you*" (Matt. 6:14, emphasis added). It's a transaction. An agreement. A price paid, if you will. Here, we're the ones who show mercy first. God follows that with his own show of mercy.

Jesus went even further in his parable of the unmerciful servant, recorded in Matthew 18:21–35.

In the parable, a king learns that one of his servants owes him a lot of money. The servant can't pay, so the king decides to sell him into slavery. The servant begs the king not to take this drastic step. Out of pity the king not only doesn't sell him but also forgives the huge debt itself.

Right after this meeting, though, the servant goes out, finds a guy who owed him money, and begins to choke him. "Pay what you owe," the servant demands. But when the other man says he hasn't got the money, the servant has him thrown in jail.

Well, the king finds out about his servant's hard heart, calls him back in, and dresses him down. "Should not you have had mercy on your fellow servant, as I had mercy on you?" the king bellows (v. 33). And he tosses the servant in prison, turning him over to "torturers," it says in some translations.

And then Jesus ended the parable with this kicker: "So also my heavenly Father will do to every one of you, if you do not forgive your brother from your heart" (v. 35).

Mercy is critical to God's character. And forgiveness is critical in the area of mercy. To truly feel God's impulse, we must be willing to forgive.

That's a hard thing to learn to do. Unimaginably hard, in some cases, as we'll talk about in the next chapter. But that's the price that *we* must pay.

God's Mercy . . . Our Mercy

The thinking side of mercy can be tricky to navigate. It requires us to engage our minds as well as our hearts—to set aside our hurt feelings and sense of justice to forgive, show mercy, and pursue a course toward what we hope will be a greater good.

That's what God did with us, after all.

Read the Bible and you'll come across plenty of verses in which God expresses his hurt and anger over our sin. And as a perfectly just God, he couldn't simply set aside his truth and righteousness.

But he found a way through. In an incredible demonstration of mercy, God forgave us.

If Christianity stands for anything, it stands for the love expressed through forgiveness. Every one of the 7.5 billion people in the world is a sinner. And every time they sin, it creates a debtor and a creditor.

We're all deep in debt—so far in debt that we can't see the top.

And yet God forgave our debts and wiped them clean.

It seems foolish, doesn't it? It's the sort of deal a businessperson would never do.

But the Bible tells us that "the foolishness of God is wiser than men, and the weakness of God is stronger than men" (1 Cor. 1:25). And, indeed, that wisdom and strength are seen through this "foolish" act of love.

About forty people wrote the Bible over about fifteen hundred years: fishermen, tax collectors, physicians, priests, and shepherds. Many had nothing in common with one another, it seems—except that they were all sinners. Some had committed deeply grievous sins against God.

And yet he used them all to tell his story—the story of his love for us. Those words still speak to us thousands of years later.

Would you use such a motley band to tell your story?

Like Tom, all these authors had betrayed God in one way or another. And yet God sat them down and said, "I've got an incredible job for you." He forgave them their sins. He used their talents. And in doing so, God was glorified.

And if we're Christians, he wants to do the same with us. He sees our potential. He knows what we can do, because he created us. He loves us. He knows we've stolen from him, cheated him, betrayed him in ways we cannot perhaps even fathom. But God takes us in his confidence anyway. He looks us in the eyes and tells us he has something he wants us to do for him.

He wants us to forgive others. Just as he forgave us. He wants us to pay the price for others, just as he paid a price for us.

For me.

I too was a traitor. I too stole—stole the gifts God had given me and used them for my own ends and I was given mercy. God gave me—us—his Son in sacrifice, making for the most one-sided transaction in the universe's history. He had all the power. I had all the sin. I could do absolutely nothing to earn my way into God's good graces. The wages—*merces*—of sin are death. I was done for.

And then, my price was paid. *Merci.*

How can we refuse to do the same for others? After all, God has a plan for them too. Maybe the first step in revealing that plan is introducing them to God's amazing calculus—to show them mercy, forgiveness—and to the "foolish" transaction that saved us all.

God's Pattern of Love for You: A Price Paid

What do you think of the well-timed offer of pardon to quell rebellion and insurrections that Alexander Hamilton proposed and which led to presidential pardons? God has not only given us this power but commanded that we use it.

Is there someone in your life whom you need to forgive right now? Have you ever accepted God's incredible offer of forgiveness?

PART 3

DO:
The Displacement of Mercy

DO JUSTICE

He went to him and bound up his wounds, pouring on oil and wine. Then he set him on his own animal and brought him to an inn and took care of him. And the next day he took out two denarii and gave them to the innkeeper. (Luke 10:34–35)

6

In the Game

*T*he Jeep rattled and jumped down the rocky road a few hours outside of Chennai, India. I held tight to a nearby grab bar, my body swaying as the vehicle lurched and growled, pushing deeper into rural India—a place left behind by the twenty-first century.

Cameras and sound equipment bounced as the Jeep made its way through the flat green landscape, palm trees swaying in the distance. Humidity clung to my clothes. The driver held the steering wheel with white knuckles as one of my companions—an attorney for the International Justice Mission (IJM)—went over our strategy again.

And then, suddenly, with a final lurch, we were there: a gray and alien crater punched in a flowing sea of green.

The heat hit me like a fist as we crawled out of the Jeep. I heard a toneless, staccato clangor—the sound of scores of hammers and chisels at work on the gray rock of the granite pit. And then I saw the workers—about a hundred of them, crouching in the dripping heat, eyes down as sweat beaded on their foreheads and necks. The men had the biggest hammers and mallets, breaking up stones through sheer repetition. Then the stones would go to the men's wives and sons and even daughters, who would break them up further with smaller tools.

"They are not allowed to leave," our guide told us.

Some call these people bonded laborers, but there's a simpler term for what they are: slaves. The cycle begins simply enough. In order to feed their families, men are forced to borrow money from quarry owners. The debtors agree to work at the quarry until they can pay back the money. But the men's wages—if they make anything at all—aren't enough to cover what the quarry owner charges for food and housing, leaving debtors in indefinite servitude.[1] Soon, in desperation, the men's wives begin working at the quarry too. Then the children. Even when the men die, the cycle goes on. Their original debts fall to their children, and their children, in perpetuity.

Such arrangements shouldn't be legal. And, in fact, they're not. But India's a massive country of more than one billion people. Most of the money it spends enforcing its laws goes to the teeming, rapidly growing cities. The country just doesn't have the resources to investigate abuses in its sprawling rural environs.

It's estimated that at least ten million people in rural India are bonded slaves. Some put the figure much higher. If a quarry owner simply admitted what was happening—if he would come clean about the incredible poverty and cycle of slavery found in these pits—the Indian government would intervene and shut the place down.

And that's one reason why I was there. The attorney from IJM suggested I play a part in this upcoming process.

We retreated to the Jeep to collect our thoughts. After a while, the attorney looked at his watch. "Well," he said, "you're up next." I got out of the vehicle. Others unstrapped the camera equipment and unpacked microphones from their cases.

Through an interpreter, I was going to interview the owner himself. If I could just get the owner to admit, on camera, what we all knew, the people hammering away in the pit could finally be free. I needed him to admit that the people here couldn't leave. That's all.

This was new territory for me. I had done plenty of negotiating in my day. But this—this was different. This wasn't just money at stake—lives were hanging in the balance.

I walked up to the middle-aged owner, a camera operator following behind me, and shook his hand. We exchanged pleasantries and began talking. I asked him about the number of quarries he owned and how many people he "employed." I asked him what happened when the workers got sick or simply wanted to go home.

We knew the truth, of course. We knew they couldn't go home. They were slaves.

But no matter how many questions I asked, the owner didn't confess. He never said an incriminating word that IJM could bring to a local magistrate.

The interview ended. As we walked back to the Jeep, I could hear again the sound of hammer on chisel, chisel on rock. *Ting-ting-ting-ting-ting.*

I had failed.

We climbed back into the Jeep and started our long drive back to Chennai. No one said a word.

Looking at the Samaritan

Mercy is risky. I've said that often in this book. To follow God's impulse, we sometimes put our finances and livelihoods at risk—even, as we saw in chapter 4, our very lives. But we also risk failure. And for some of us, that is the most difficult risk of all.

We're at step three in our four-step process in God's "pattern of love." In the first part of the book, we talked about how important it is to see and feel. In the second, we talked about the next step: go and discover the facts of a situation. We must make a conscious decision to walk toward a merciful endeavor, just as the Samaritan did. And we must take that decision seriously, even to the point where we might take an off-ramp if we feel so led.

But after we see and after we go, we come to perhaps the most critical point of all: we must *do*. We truly step out in faith and try to accomplish something remarkable through mercy. Doing always involves a complicated word—*displacement*. The minute we get on someone else's agenda, they are in need of our resources and we serve them with love. We end up with displaced priorities, schedules, resources, and hearts. This idea of displacement has deep truth. Henri Nouwen writes, "It is urgent that we reclaim this great tradition of displacement . . . it leads to compassion; by bringing us closer to our brokenness it opens our eyes to our fellow human beings, who seek our consolation and comfort." He then makes a bone-rattling comment: we then "disappear as an object of interest."[2]

Servanthood makes us "disappear," because when we diminish ourselves, it is easier to have fellowship and love others. In business and in life, so often we try to build a resume that makes us different and remarkable. Displacement reverses this process.

Doing anything, particularly anything worthwhile, also involves the risk of failure. I compare it to marching up to bat in a baseball game. You *see* the pitcher. You *feel* the bat in your hand. You *go* to the plate. But then, when the pitch starts screaming your way, you have to *do* something with it. You have to swing.

Guess what? You don't make contact all the time. Not in baseball, and not in life. Your startup business could go bankrupt. Your novel could fall flat. Your diet could be a bust. Change is hard—be it changing yourself, your environment, or your world.

When the Good Samaritan went to the injured traveler, he was taking a risk. What if bandits were lying in wait for someone to help the guy? What if the man died at the inn anyway? What if the innkeeper overcharged him? What if this? What if that? The Samaritan had no guarantee that everything would work out just fine. In fact, it's interesting where Jesus left his story: with the man, still grievously injured, at the inn. We don't hear that the traveler made a full recovery. We don't know whether the traveler went on to become a good, generous leader in his community. Jesus didn't offer us a typical "happily ever after" conclusion or a satisfying "where are they now" coda.

But we know how the story would've ended had the Samaritan not acted. It would've ended with a dead, broken man lying in a ditch. Because the Samaritan followed the three steps of God's impulse—see, go, and do—mercy was manifested. Because the Samaritan took a chance, the traveler had a chance.

As we move from the disposition of our heart (chapters 2 and 3) to the discovery of mercy (chapters 4 and 5), we are now at the point of justice—doing, serving, and being displaced. The Samaritan perfectly embodies justice by both protecting and providing for his enemy. Think of what our world would look like if we allowed our mercy to grow into individual and systemic justice.

Brazilian lyricist and novelist Paul Coelho once said, "There is only one thing that makes a dream impossible to achieve: the fear of failure."[3] When we're scared to fail, we don't do anything. We don't try. We're stuck in the batter's box, afraid to take a swing.

That's not the way God wants us to live. God put us on this earth not to be afraid of failure, not to take up space, but to do something. So let's look again at the Samaritan and examine more closely what he did.

First, the Samaritan bandaged the man's wounds. I doubt that travelers back in Jesus's day carried around packages of Band-Aids and packets of gauze. The Samaritan probably tore up one of his own garments or perhaps a bit of cloth he had planned to sell elsewhere. He poured oil and wine on the wounds—again, pricey stuff back in the day, merchandise worth treasuring and trading. And then the Samaritan took the traveler to an inn and gave the innkeeper two denarii for the man's room and board.

The Samaritan didn't simply give up his first and best, he was flat-out generous. A silver denarii—the coin of the realm in ancient Rome—would've been enough to keep the traveler there for two or three weeks. And remember, the Samaritan spent that first night caring for this beaten man himself. That's the very definition of hands-on care.

Jesus used this parable to show us what biblical love for our neighbor (and enemy!) should really look like. It involves the Samaritan's eyes (see). It engages his emotions (feel). It concerns his mind and judgment, guiding him whether he should go. And here it affects his will, giving everything necessary to help not just a man but a stranger—and someone who might well view him as a hated, untouchable enemy.

Feel free to go back to that sidebar in chapter 1 for a moment. It's good to remember that this parable began with a religious leader asking about how he might obtain eternal life. He understood, and rightly, the part about loving God with all his heart, soul, mind, and strength. But he was a little "foggy" about who his neighbor was. Jesus pulls off what Pastor Tim Keller would call a theological "reverse trap." He turns the presumed hero of the story—the theological elite—into the story's uncaring villain. The Samaritan, whom Jews had been trained to think of as the bad guy, is the hero. Keller writes, "Our Lord attacks the complacency of comfortably religious people who protect themselves from the needs of others."[4]

And in that surprising Samaritan, we see all the aspects of what we'd expect to show God in worship—not the singing, clapping worship of church but worship as God intended in all its fullness, the generous, wholehearted love encompassing all we have and are. And it was all for an enemy.

In a sense, the Samaritan story foreshadows Christ's own work on the cross. His act was the ultimate act of generosity.

He was mocked, beaten, and eventually killed. And then Jesus went ahead and saved his abusers and killers.

Jesus took the ultimate risk for us. And it's up to us to validate that risk.

Outsourced Compassion

Human beings, as a rule, don't like risk. We hate failure—especially when it can look us right in the eye.

Ironically, I think that's one reason we have so many non-profit organizations today.

More than 1.6 million nonprofits operate in the United States.[5] That's 9 percent of our national economy. According to the National Council of Nonprofits, if you took nonprofit organizations out of the overall economy and pretended they made up a country of their own, nonprofits would be the sixteenth largest economy in the world.[6]

Yes, these nonprofits are a blessing. And yet they're not a blessing.

I know, I know. Some of you are probably saying, "Huh?" Let me explain.

In business, we regularly use the term "partner." We may find financial partners, operating partners, strategic partners, and equity partners. Why do we partner with them? Pretty simple, really. Our partners have the ability or resources to do things that we, by ourselves, can't do. Someone may have a great idea for a small business, but they have no capital. So they seek out a financial partner to help them out. Another person may have plenty of capital and a desire to invest, but they don't know the first thing about the particular business. So they seek out an operating partner to handle the nuts and bolts of the business.

That's sometimes true in the world of charity as well. Sometimes we need experts to facilitate the change we want to enact and the mercy we want to give.

But more often it's not about our lacking the expertise. We have nonprofit or ministry partners who do things we either don't want to do or don't have the time to do. When we don't want to go and do, they go and do for us.

These organizations are usually well-intentioned. And the government (also well-intentioned) makes it easy for us to give. Sections 501(c)(3) and (4) of the IRS tax code specifically promote charitable giving, allowing tax deductions for a whole battery of causes and initiatives. Donate to help the poor or underprivileged? That's a tax deduction. Want to use your money to advance science, religion, or education? Ditto. Want to donate some cash to construct a public building? You'll get a healthy tax break on that one. In 2016, Americans gave more than $390 billion to charities—the most generous we've ever been.[7] In 2015, about 62.6 million people volunteered to "make a difference." And most of those opportunities were made possible through our vibrant nonprofit sector.

But as good as all this might seem, and as much positive change as those organizations can help facilitate, some believe this booming nonprofit economy may not be as healthy as it first appears. They believe it has two problems.

1. Efficiency

A few years ago, a woman approached me to talk about an organization she ran—a service to fight child illiteracy here in Atlanta. It sounded like a wonderful program. Volunteers would meet with students every week and read to them, thus helping them get familiar with words and books and the joy of reading. But as we talked, I wondered whether her efforts were duplicating those of other organizations. So I asked her how many programs in Atlanta were geared toward reducing illiteracy.

"About fifteen," she said.

After our talk, I did a quick search on the internet and found 287 organizations that deal with childhood illiteracy in Atlanta alone.

Now, maybe all these organizations are absolutely necessary. Maybe each of them deals with the issue in their own unique way and thus serves a unique niche. But when I look at those numbers as a businessman, a couple of words pop into my head: *oversaturation* and *duplication*. I have to wonder whether many of those organizations are doing the exact same thing, thus cannibalizing their own work and needlessly replicating their efforts to no one's greater good.

Carburetors are important, but you don't buy a car with 287 carburetors under the hood. It's wasted effort. You don't look at a city block with 287 burger joints on it and decide to build one more.

In 2013, Peter Buffett, son of billionaire Warren Buffett, wrote a scathing critique of what he called the "charitable industrial complex" for the *New York Times*. He notes that, even as the number of nonprofits keeps growing, the problems never seem to shrink. Inequality remains. He calls for systemic change to a system that, he believes, primarily serves as a "conscience salve" to the rich who want to give back but actually does very little to impact human suffering. [8]

"It's time for a new operating system," Buffett writes. "Not a 2.0 or a 3.0, but something built from the ground up. New code."[9] My friend Bob Lupton says that the existing system perpetrates "poverty maintenance." Just enough is done for the poor to keep them poor.

2. Relationality

Even if we brush aside concerns about efficiency, we're still losing something when we outsource our compassion. We lose the essence of mercy, and this lack of relational connectivity is my primary concern.

Back in Jesus's day, if you wanted to help someone, you helped them. Jesus and his disciples saw the people they healed; they touched them. To show mercy back then, you had to see and feel, go and do. You didn't have much of an alternative.

But over the centuries, layers of bureaucracy have been overlaid on mercy. We hand over the task to deacons and volunteers, then to committees and companies. We pay someone else to go and do for us. If we have trouble seeing because we have our heads down like sheep, and we have trouble feeling with our eight-second attention spans, then we outsource our compassion—often by writing checks—rather than going. When it comes to serving and doing, who wants to be displaced?

Let me remind you of a couple of the stats I mentioned earlier. The United States gave more than $390 billion to nonprofits in 2016—the most ever. About 62.6 million people donated their time, which represents another step in a decade-long decline.[10] We're giving more but serving less.

Experts are mystified by this dichotomy. Why is giving increasing while volunteering is decreasing? It doesn't make sense, they say. "What don't we see?" writes Tess Srebro for *Engaging Volunteers*. "We don't see the why."[11]

The answer lies in our failure to understand what mercy's really all about.

Mercy isn't always served by writing a check. Yes, good works can come about through our financial generosity, but this isn't mercy. It's Peter Buffett's "conscience salve." To understand God's impulse, we need to know the people we want to help. We need to see whom we're serving. *Relational* generosity is where justice and love begin.

Why are people giving more and serving less? One reason might be rooted in fear. We're afraid of looking the world's need in the eye. We're afraid of being fully confronted with the pain and suffering of a broken world. We're afraid of that sort of raw intimacy. And we're afraid of failing. When we outsource our compassion, we can comfort ourselves in the thought that, *Hey, at least we tried to do something. If it fails, it's not because of us.*

But when we go out into this frightening world and try to do something, the possibility of failure stares us in the face. That's terrifying.

Earlier I said a key to mercy was context. *What's their story?* I asked.

When we truly engage in mercy—when we take this third step in the pattern of love—we enter into someone's story, as messy and uncomfortable as it may feel at first. We're getting close to someone. We're entering a place of spiritual intimacy.

And there's another fear too.

To engage in relational mercy—to see and feel, go, and do—means we might not just enact a little change in a hurting world, but *we* might change too. When we're merciful, we open ourselves up to feeling like we've never felt before.

And it's not just love we feel; we also feel rage. Rage at the world's most horrific injustices.

Structural Injustice

Dee is an absolute delight.

She's the daughter of someone very close to me—a young, married, professional woman who excels at her job and is highly educated. God blessed Dee with a great mind and fantastic attitude.

But when I talk with her, my heart breaks a little. Not for her but for the millions like her who never got the same chance.

Dee was born in Chennai, India, not too far away from the gravel pit I mentioned. My friend adopted her. Had she grown up in Chennai, her life would be defined by one word: untouchable.

India's millennia-old caste system is technically illegal, but it still holds amazing sway over the country's culture. Developed by the dominant priestly class (called Brahmins) around 900 BC, it was part of an early stage of Hinduism. The caste system was represented as a body: the learned priests were depicted as the head of Indian society. Government leaders and members of the military were the arms while businesspeople were seen as the thighs. The illiterate and those unfit for greater responsibility were the feet—the untouchables.

But even though these body parts were identified by occupation, people were born into the caste system. Brahmins were born to be Brahmins. The illiterate stayed illiterate. And if by some odd twist of fate a member of the untouchable caste learned to read? It didn't matter. They were still untouchable. In addition, the caste system stems from a religion that says part of a person's failures today come from the failures of their *prior lives*—lives that obviously a person can't do anything about in the here and now. It's as if everyone's lot in life is preordained.

A farmer commits suicide every thirty minutes, in part due to the hopelessness of this supposedly outlawed system. I have spent ten years helping their widows. It breaks my heart.

Structural injustice is difficult enough to deal with. As mentioned above, when it has its underpinnings in religion, changing it becomes even more daunting. In the book *Broken People,* author Smita Narula and Human Rights Watch Asia document the terrible abuse perpetrated on the 160 million people who make up the untouchables.

Because of my relationship with Dee, that injustice strikes painfully close to home.

It makes me angry—angry to think of the millions upon millions of people like Dee who'll never get the chance to follow in her footsteps. They may be equally smart and equally talented. But they'll never go to college. Never have a chance to work their way out of crushing poverty. They can't because they're not allowed to. Millions are cut off by an entire society, with next-to-no chance of escaping. Like the men and women in the granite pit, they're trapped. Enslaved.

They're not allowed to leave.

Does it make you mad when you see such a rigged, grossly unfair system? Does it make you want to go and do something? My involvement in India has changed me. It has shown me the huge injustices millions of Indian people face because of the backward caste system. Danger, discrimination, and the utter loss of freedom haunt them. I've seen modern-day slaves work in the granite pits. I've heard of women and even children forced into prostitution.

And yet the global community seems strangely silent. How odd that we can campaign tirelessly to save the environmental habitat of a mouse but won't insist on changing a system like this that stunts humanity itself—a system that threatens millions of people's health and homes, their livelihoods and their very lives.

And don't imagine for a minute that India's the only place such injustices exist. Institutional injustice reigns around the globe. Even here in the United States, we still smell that stench of societal discrimination. We're burdened by centuries-old history. The "New World" was supposed to be better than the Old, but the same problems followed us here. I suspect that I've had opportunities that simply would've never opened up for me if I'd been born with a different skin color.

As we try to follow God's impulse, we need to remember those two key facets of God himself: mercy and justice. When we see systems like the ones in India, we should follow God's lead and respond in kind—showering mercy on the oppressed. We should feel inside ourselves a desire for justice for the oppressors. As Bishop Alexander said, it's not necessarily our fault. But it is our problem.

Pursuing Justice

When we enter into this third step of God's impulse, the do, mercy is inextricably linked to justice. The prophet Micah writes that the Lord requires us "to *do* justly, and to *love* mercy, and to walk humbly with thy God" (Mic. 6:8 KJV, emphasis added). We're supposed to act in accordance with God's perfect justice, even as we try to show mercy to God's imperfect creations.

Will Herberg, a twentieth-century Jewish theologian, once said, "Justice is the institutionalization of love."[12] When we build our systems to love the least of us, we have hope to manifest love. But structural injustice is everywhere. And when we pursue God's impulse, we often find it difficult to see what his impulse really looks like.

I'm on the board of a ministry that has a very basic tenet: never help people who can help themselves. There's a difference between a crisis and a chronic problem, they say. The ministry's here to help people in immediate distress—people who are drowning in crisis and need a hand to pull them up. But helping people in chronic distress, the ministry believes, is somehow perpetuating the problem.

I get that. And it's true—except when it's not.

Structural injustices are the fly in the ointment of my ministry's tenet. It sounds so obvious, until you step past your own life and background and see society through someone else's eyes. When you do that, this neatly packaged solution doesn't feel so neat.

Take Joyce, a friend of mine. As a nurse's aide, Joyce makes $13 an hour. If she worked forty hours a week, she'd make a living wage. Barely.

But Joyce rarely works forty hours a week—not because she doesn't want to, but because she can't. It's not unusual for Joyce's employer to call her up at the beginning of the week and say they'll only need her for, say, four days instead of five. Or three. For Joyce, one phone call could equal anywhere from a 20 to 40 percent pay cut for the week.

Then, after several weeks of less-than-expected pay, the rent comes due. Where does she turn to for help? Not to that ministry I mentioned. After all, her crisis looks chronic. But is she at fault? I don't think so. The fault lies with the system.

We fight over what constitutes a living wage—defined as what one needs to earn to support a minimally acceptable lifestyle. According to the National Low Income Housing Coalition, the current minimum wage falls far short of that. There's not a region in the country where you can rent a two-bedroom apartment with a $7.25-an-hour job. Renting a one-bedroom apartment is doable—in only twelve counties in the entire country. If you're a single mom here in Atlanta with two kids and you need a two-bedroom apartment, you'd need to earn $18.25 an hour or put in one hundred–hour workweeks in a minimum-wage job.[13]

What responsibility do we have to workers who get paid $7 or $8 an hour? I've never heard a pastor speak on the subject. I've never seen a church address it.

I think we should. Mercy and justice go hand in hand. We need to embrace hard questions about what policies and initiatives have been in place that contribute to chronic poverty and a lack of education. Our hearts of mercy must be incensed over individual and systemic injustices. As Dietrich Bonhoeffer said, "We are not to simply bandage the wounds of victims beneath the wheels of injustice, we are to drive a spoke into the wheel itself."[14]

The Reward of Failure

The God Impulse is hard to follow. When we enter into this third step of the process, we sometimes find roadblocks everywhere. The problems can feel overwhelming. Injustice, particularly institutional injustice, seems almost impossible to combat. We face our own doubts. Our own fears. *What if I fail?* we think to ourselves.

Sometimes it seems easiest to not even try.

I think about the Samaritan, leaning beside that broken traveler. Snapped bones, perhaps. Blood everywhere. The man was half dead; it wouldn't take much to push him all the way.

It must've been bewildering to look at the man's injuries. He didn't have a medic to triage the situation. *Where do I start?* the Samaritan might've wondered. So many urgent needs, so little time.

But he tackled the situation anyway. The Samaritan's mercy wasn't dammed by doubts or fears or anger. It flowed.

Mercy's tough. Frustrating. We have no guarantee of success.

But you know something? Even when we fail, God can work through us anyway.

I still remember how defeated I felt as we drove away from that granite quarry, where so many men, women, and children were working against their will. I had failed them. The pit in my stomach was so big, it felt as though I had swallowed a rock.

But while that part of my trip felt like a failure, the rest of it did not.

I visited rural job training facilities that were preparing girls and women who'd been freed from forced prostitution for other jobs. I saw ministries across rural India determined to help the country's poor and threatened in dozens of different ways. It was beautiful.

Then, months after I returned to Atlanta, I got a call from our host.

"You're not going to believe this," he said.

The quarry owner had just been arrested. The quarry had been turned over to the workers themselves. They were free! They became their own bosses. They could stay home if they were sick. Their children might have a chance to get an education. And to top it off, local Christians had reached out to the quarry workers and a number of them had become Christians themselves. Hallelujah!

Yes, I failed. But God had not.

I can't tell you whether my failed attempt to get the owner talking was one small piece in this glorious story. I don't know what part, if any, I played in God's work there.

But I was part of the story, even if I was just a small part. If the third step in this process of mercy is like swinging a bat in a baseball game, I felt like I had gone 0-for-4. But you know what? I was still on the winning team.

I learned something from my experience there. It reminded me that, as much as God wants us to put in our best efforts, he's not totally dependent on what we do. And to me, that's almost a relief. We may fail. We may even feel like we've failed God at times. But it's important to remember that God *never* fails.

When we follow God's impulse, we must see. We must go. We must do. But nowhere does it say we must succeed. Ultimately, God has that covered. And in that, I rejoice.

God's Pattern of Love for You: Displacement

Tim Keller calls servanthood "the operating system of Christianity." True service requires displacement. This is a hard idea. We need to understand that God promises to bless us as we bless others.

Is there someone who God is calling you to love and serve? Are you willing to go beyond where you live, work, and play?

7

Hallelujah

DIVINE MERCY FOR OUR ENEMIES

Her name was Lola, and she was a slave.

Lola didn't toil in the Alabama cotton fields 150 years ago or work out of a God-forsaken brothel halfway around the world. The four-foot-eleven woman lived most of her life in American suburbs and died in 2011. And yet according to a story published in *The Atlantic* by the Pulitzer Prize–winning journalist Alex Tizon, she was a slave as sure as if she had been bound in irons.[1]

She was a "gift" to Alex's mother from her father, Lt. Tom Asuncion, when they lived in the Philippines in 1943 and such arrangements were not uncommon. When Alex's mom got married and moved to America, Lola came too, lured by the promise of pay that never came. For more than fifty years, she cooked and cleaned for Alex's family. She often slept on piles of dirty laundry.

Lola never left the Tizons. She couldn't. She had no money, no legal ID. She'd been abused, verbally and occasionally physically. Alex's mom yelled at and berated her often.

And then, in the late 1990s, Alex's mother got leukemia.

Lola could've exacted revenge for all those years of slavery and abuse, but she did the opposite. She cared for Alex's mother throughout her last difficult days, sitting beside her bedside, holding a cup filled with water, a straw at the ready, to give to her if she was ever thirsty.

When the end came close, a Catholic priest visited to perform last rites. He asked Alex's mother if there was anything she needed to forgive—and anything she needed to be forgiven for. Alex writes: "She scanned the room with heavy-lidded eyes, said nothing. Then, without looking at Lola, she reached over and placed an open hand on her head. She didn't say a word."

Two women together at the threshold of death, bound together for more than fifty years by an unimaginable secret.

Lola could've hated Alex's mother. Lola could've killed her herself and some might've called it justice. Instead, Lola cared for the woman as her last weeks shrank to days, then hours. "She had become extra attentive to my mother, and extra kind," Alex writes.

Lola gives us a picture of unimaginable mercy, beautiful and inexplicable and scandalous. And it forces us to ask an impossible question to answer: If I were Lola, would I have done the same? A heart of mercy can help us see and react to policies and attitudes that contribute to racism and injustice.

The Soaring Mercy of Forgiveness

"To err is human, to forgive, divine," writes Alexander Pope.[2] I believe that's true. Loving and forgiving our enemies are the ultimate divine expressions in life.

The pattern of love is difficult to follow. It can be easy to see and feel mercy, particularly for those who seem to deserve and need it. It can be more difficult to go into mercy—to reconcile with those who don't seem so deserving. We don't always feel it then; it takes effort to follow God's impulse.

But this third step—to truly know what it is to do mercy—means making yet another difficult move. We cross the threshold beyond helping the needy or serving the poor and enter the realm of forgiveness. And that, for some, can be a tough realm to enter.

On the cross, Jesus cried out to the Father, imploring him to forgive his killers: "They know not what they do" (Luke 23:34). Christianity's first martyr, Stephen, begged God to forgive his own murderers as they stoned him. "Lord," he said, "do not hold this sin against them" (Acts 7:60).

Saul of Tarsus watched as Stephen's accusers stoned him. The Pharisee was educated, brilliant, devout, and one of Christendom's most zealous early persecutors. Did he smirk as Stephen died? Stare on in stony silence? The Bible doesn't say. But it does place him at the scene—he heard Stephen's words of forgiveness as the rocks pounded the saint's body. Perhaps he remembered Stephen's forgiveness later when he became a Christian. Regardless, Saul—who became the great evangelist Paul—understood the depth of the forgiveness shown to him, both divine and temporal.

He writes in 1 Timothy 1:13, "Even though I was once a blasphemer and a persecutor and a violent man, I was shown mercy because I acted in ignorance and unbelief" (NIV).

The key word here is *once*, by the way. Saul acted out of ignorance. As Jesus said, he knew not what he did. But God knew; he saw the person who Saul could become. He looked past Saul's horrific deeds and recognized his potential, the beauty and purpose he had given the man. What great mercy that God looked at Saul's being complicit in Stephen's murder and called him ignorant. That God gave him a new name, Paul, and a new mission and let him peer into the third heaven. We should not wonder why Paul was motivated.

He deserved worse, but God gave him something better.

"For as the heavens are higher than the earth, so are my ways higher than your ways and my thoughts than your thoughts" (Isa. 55:9). God's heavenly ways allowed Paul's passion, knowledge, and commitment to be redirected. He became a chosen vessel.

"Sin is a wound," writes Pope Francis in *The Name of God Is Mercy*. "It needs to be treated, to be healed."[3]

With mercy, anyone can be a vessel for God. A corrupt politician. A crooked banker. An ISIS fighter. Yes, even a killer who beheads Christians on a beach can be saved and used through God's love. He could find the road to forgiveness on God's highest bridge.

And the same could be said for our enemies. God can bridge a seemingly impossible gorge and make life very different—for them and for us.

Mercy's Third Way

In this book, we've talked already about two rich aspects of mercy—ways in which we can see more clearly this critical aspect of God's character and understand why God thinks it's so important that we embrace it ourselves.

In the first part of our book, we saw mercy through its Hebrew root *racham*, which shares some similarity with the Hebrew word for womb. Through this understanding, we provide warmth, care, and protection to the poor and distressed.

In the second part, we examined mercy through its Latin word, *merced*, meaning price paid. We know that we don't always feel like being merciful. But in many cases, mercy simply makes sense; it's just good business. We talked about mercy's calculus and cost, and we acknowledged that even though God wants us to show mercy whenever we can, sometimes the cost could simply be too much.

Now, we come to the most difficult but most beautiful expression of mercy we have: the divine power of mercy through forgiveness, even in the face of the weightiest of sins.

The reality is more complicated than I'm about to suggest, of course, and these steps can overlap significantly.

The first step, the desire to provide a womb for those suffering or in need, is an *emotional* impulse. We feel the need, and so we want to act on it.

The second is *intellectual*. We may not feel the impulse, but rationally, we can see its benefit and weigh its costs and dividends.

The third lands us in more rarified *spiritual* territory. We may not feel like forgiving our enemies. We may not see any practical reason for doing so. But we still hear God calling us to build a bridge of mercy to someone; a difficult, maybe even painful bridge, but a bridge they need—and perhaps we need too. When we follow God's impulse through forgiveness, we're leaning on his divine understanding of mercy, not our own. It's only through his help that we can build the bridge across the gorge.

To illustrate the dynamics of this, let's return to my area of expertise: business.

When someone sins against someone else, that's a spiritual transaction. The one who's done the sinning is, morally speaking, in someone else's debt. The one who has been sinned against has, if you forgive the term, an "asset" on their ledger—something that can often be used against the debtor as leverage to recoup their losses.

But when someone forgives a moral debt, they're simply "writing off" this asset and wiping it away.

We're all in need of forgiveness when it comes to God. We're in debt up to our scalps. And yet when we're in communion with God, he forgives us. He writes off our debts. God says in Hebrews 8:12, "For I will be merciful toward their iniquities, and I will remember their sins no more."

That's forgiveness. That's an incredible expression of love.

In Paul's famous chapter on love in 1 Corinthians 13, we hear how love does not keep track of sin and moral debt. It does not tabulate the wrongs suffered. "Love bears all things, believes all things, hopes all things, endures all things," Paul writes in verse 7. When it comes to love, forgiveness is critical.

These three sides of mercy—feeling, thinking, and divine (or if you'd rather, emotional, intellectual, and spiritual)—are absolutely critical to understanding God's character and following his impulse. It is like the threefold cord we read about in Ecclesiastes 4:12: it is not easily broken.

Make no mistake, to forgive—to truly follow this divine aspect of mercy—is hard, sometimes unimaginably hard.

But it can be done. God showed us how. And one of the purest pictures of forgiveness and divine mercy can be found, believe it or not, on Broadway.

Playing God

Many experts believe *Les Misérables* is one of the greatest books ever written. Penned by Victor Hugo and published in 1862, it was transformed into a musical in 1980 and has run continually on London's famed West End since 1985. It's been a staple on Broadway as well and was adapted into an Oscar-nominated film in 2012.

Les Misérables is my favorite Broadway play. Between the play and the movie, I have seen it five times. It's a powerful demonstration of this divine type of mercy.

The musical opens in prison, focusing on the pitiful Jean Valjean—locked up, in essence, for stealing a loaf of bread to feed his sister and her seven starving children.

Valjean is finally released nineteen years after that initial infraction. But in nineteenth-century France (where the story takes place), former convicts were practically unemployable—the equivalent of an Indian untouchable.

Valjean eventually stumbles into a church, and the bishop offers him food and shelter. But the former con, embittered by his experience, has turned savage and selfish. During the night when no one's looking, Valjean takes the church's precious silver.

Valjean doesn't get very far before he's caught. He desperately—and lamely—says the bishop gave him the silverware, but the constables certainly know a lie when they hear one. They drag Valjean back to the church and ask for the bishop's confirmation—a confirmation they know won't be coming.

But then, to the surprise of the constables and especially Valjean, the bishop says he did give the silver to the former convict. And then the bishop says something even more remarkable:

> But my friend, you left so early
> Surely something slipped your mind.
> You forget I gave these also—
> Would you leave the best behind?[4]

Then the bishop hands Valjean a pair of exquisite, incredibly valuable candlesticks.

The audience gasps each time at the bishop's outrageous act of mercy. It's almost unthinkable, even scandalous. And given the reaction, perhaps it's not so surprising that they miss what the bishop whispers in Valjean's ear afterward:

> God has raised you out of darkness:
> I have bought your soul for God![5]

With that line, the bishop walks into the "divine" side of mercy. In a sense, he steps into the role of God, showering Valjean with a godlike forgiveness and giving him a second chance.

Had the bishop taken a hard "truth" stance in this moment, Valjean would've likely been sent to prison for the rest of his life. Perhaps worse. He would've been punished as the law demands, and his life would've been wasted as a result.

Instead, the bishop challenges Valjean to use the money from the silver to make a life for himself. That's just what Valjean does—showering his own form of mercy and generosity on those who cross his path.

When we practice mercy like the bishop, we also have a chance to "play God." Just think, in every act of mercy with a fellow sinner or an enemy, we have a chance to weigh the offense against the value of their soul, just as the bishop did. *I have bought your soul for God.* It gives me goosebumps.

According to Proverbs 19:11, it's our glory to "overlook an offense." Such a powerful word that is—*glory*. In Psalm 8:5, we're told that God "crowned [humanity] with glory and honor." The Bible tells us that, yes, we are glory-filled creations naturally, made in the *Imago Dei*. But as we've already talked about, God is merciful and forgiving. When we overlook people's sins, faults, and insults, we are living up to the godlike, glorious image God has placed within us and our own sin has tried so furiously to erase.

We are made in God's image. But we never look more like him as when we're merciful.

The Bible emphasizes again and again how integral mercy is to who God is. Even Jesus points it out.

We look to Jesus as our model—the one "full of truth and grace" who obviously performed the ultimate demonstration of mercy on the cross. Jesus is our template for most things—except mercy. When it comes to that one trait, Jesus points to God himself. "Be merciful, even as your Father is merciful," he says in Luke 6:36. Jesus points upward and says, "Look at my Father."

It's not that Jesus wasn't merciful. Of course he was. But when we look at God, we see that the universe itself is writ in his mercy—from the beginning to now to the end of time. God's merciful impulse sent his beloved Son to be a sacrifice for us. In Revelation 13:8, we read about a book written "before the foundation of the world," and it's "the book of life of the Lamb who was slain."

Our loving Creator knew we would misuse the freedom he gave us to live and love. He knew he'd need a plan B, which was through mercy and the sacrifice of his Son—"his one and only Son" (John 3:16 NIV). With that sacrifice, he built a bridge for us, a bridge that led directly to him and away from the enemy.

"To love another person is to see the face of God," as stated in the musical version of *Les Misérables*. In some respects, loving another is to play God in the best possible way.

But what happens when *we're* the enemy of mercy? What do we do then?

The Institutional Sin of Racism

For years, South African politician Adriaan Vlok was more than a cog in the country's tragic machine of apartheid. He was its engine.

He became South Africa's minister of law and order in 1985, in charge of protecting the racist system of apartheid and maintaining the country's white rule. Around thirty thousand people were detained during his reign of terror. Many of them were kidnapped; some were tortured, drugged, and even killed. One unit under his authority once forced a handful of young anti-apartheid activists into a bus filled with explosives and pushed it off a cliff.[6]

Still, the rage against apartheid, both within South Africa and around the world, was growing. Activists grew increasingly outspoken, and South Africa's racist regime grew more desperate. Volk took special notice of Frank Chikane, a charismatic black Christian preacher and tireless opponent of apartheid. Vlok decided he had to go.

In 1989, two of Vlok's policemen secretly went to the Johannesburg airport while Chikane was there traveling to Namibia, burgled his suitcase, and poisoned his underwear with insecticide. The plot nearly worked; Chikane grew deathly ill and was flown to the United States for treatment.

But such cloak-and-dagger machinations weren't enough to save a government not worth saving. Despite all Vlok's efforts, apartheid would crumble and fall. Vlok was forced out in 1991. His wife committed suicide in 1995, and many suspect Vlok himself might've been tempted to follow suit.[7]

But he didn't. Instead, Vlok wrestled with his legacy and his faith. Christian evangelists asked Vlok to join their movement—become the hands and feet of God. Build bridges to others. Vlok protested that he'd done terrible things. Unspeakable things. But the evangelists pointed to the Bible—to Moses, who killed an Egyptian. To David, the adulterer. They told him God could still use him. And finally, Vlok believed it to be so.[8]

But Vlok still felt chained to his past. He'd not been convicted of a crime—except by himself.

In 2006, the former government minister walked into his old workplace to see Frank Chikane, who was now working for the government himself. Even as Chikane smiled warmly at Vlok, the former minister began to shake. He couldn't speak. Instead, he handed Chikane a Bible with a written message on the front flyleaf.

"I have sinned against the Lord and against you!" the message read. "Will you forgive me?" And then Vlok opened his briefcase and took out a bowl and a rag.

"Frank, please, would you allow me to wash your feet?"

Chikane, somewhat stunned, allowed him to do so.

By the time the small ceremony was over, both men were in tears.

For some, the foot washing was simply a publicity stunt. That Vlok has spent the last decade feeding South Africa's poor isn't enough either—not nearly enough to wash away the evil he did.[9] For white Afrikaners, many of whom are afraid of South Africa's majority black government, Vlok is a traitor. One writer called him a "quivering dog."[10]

But for Vlok, the criticism is moot and the work continues. According to a 2015 article in the *Mail & Guardian*, he shares a house with a black furniture repairman, a convicted murderer, and a white family that was previously homeless. He spends his days handing out food to poor black families in the township of Olievenhoutbosch.[11]

"I regarded myself as better than black people," Vlok admitted to the *New Republic* in 2014. "More intelligent. I work harder. I thought to myself all the time: 'I am better than you.' . . . And it is wrong! It is not so! [When I washed Chikane's feet,] I saw that I'm not better than they are. . . . I started looking at black people through different eyes, because feet-washing put me in the place of the slave."[12]

Vlok was forgiven by some of the very same people he had persecuted. For some, such forgiveness is scandalous—a miscarriage of justice. But when I see that story, I see something else at work: the God Impulse.

The Logs in Our Own Eyes

The United States bears some of the same scars that South Africa does. Even as Thomas Jefferson wrote, "All men are created equal," inequality was everywhere, even at Jefferson's own southern plantation.

Bishop Alexander, speaking at Venture Christian Church in Silicon Valley in 2017, said, "Racism is in the ground of our country. It is in the very fact and fiber in the forming documents."[13] And indeed it is.

For a hundred years, the New World's colonies bought, sold, and imported other human beings, codifying their ownership into law. For another hundred years, a young, idealistic nation turned its back to the evils of slavery. In the Supreme Court's infamous Dred Scott decision in 1857, Chief Justice Roger Taney said that black men "had no rights which the white man was bound to respect."[14]

The Emancipation Proclamation theoretically freed the slaves in slave states in 1863, and the Civil War and a flurry of laws inculcated that freedom—technically. But less than twenty years later, Jim Crow laws began codifying a discriminatory social order that rubbed yet more salt into the nation's racial wounds, reinforced, as Alexander says, "by violence and intimidation."[15] From 1882 to 1968, nearly four thousand African Americans were lynched—killed for no reason other than their skin color.[16] Nationally, laws, codes, and subsidies ensured that African Americans would remain at a social and financial disadvantage.

By the 1960s, those discriminatory laws were finally being dismantled. Tremendous strides have been made since that time, and yet racial tensions persist. The Black Lives Matter movement is proof of that.

"The matter of race is not our fault," Alexander told a mostly white congregation. "But it is our problem. We have inherited the blessing and burdens of race in America."[17]

Alexander said the issue of race is something the church is uniquely equipped to address. The church, like the Good Samaritan, could be a womb—a safe place of healing and restoration. It could be a bridge, allowing people of different races and ethnicities to truly find communion with one another.

But all too often the church has not been that womb. Sometimes instead of building bridges on this issue, it's torn them down.

Largely because of their support of slavery, Southern Baptist churches split from the North in 1845. After the Civil War and into the civil rights era, the Southern Baptist Convention was instrumental in keeping the races as separate as possible. Historian and former Southern Baptist Wayne Flynt says that "the church was the last bastion of segregation."[18] Only in 1995 did the Convention renounce its racist past.[19] The Presbyterian Church of America voted to do the same in 2016.

But apologies can never completely heal the wounds of the past. Only time can do that. And even then, the scars can remain.

In 2017, I was invited to speak at a prayer breakfast in Birmingham, Alabama. The invitation was followed by a request for me to talk at a racial reconciliation lunch the same day.

I felt wholly inadequate.

Birmingham was probably the most segregated city in America in the early 1960s and the epicenter for the sometimes-violent struggle for civil rights. On Birmingham streets, police sprayed African American high schoolers with high-pressure hoses and attacked them with dogs when the youths tried to peacefully march to city hall. The city had so many unsolved bombings that it was called "Bombingham."

Many local churches sat back and did nothing. Indeed, in an open letter, eight Alabama pastors laid the blame of civil unrest at the feet of the protesters.

When Martin Luther King Jr. was arrested in Birmingham on April 16, 1963, he wrote a scathing indictment of the church. He confessed that he had once hoped—believed—that predominantly white churches would back his moral, faith-driven quest for equality. Like Alexander, he believed he was equipped to be a catalyst for positive change. Instead, King wrote, "Some have been outright opponents, refusing to understand the freedom movement and misrepresenting its leaders; all too many others have been more cautious than courageous and have remained silent behind the anesthetizing security of stained glass windows."[20]

As I pondered the invitation to speak in Birmingham, I wondered, *How could a white man like me address this issue?* I don't know what it's like to be stopped on the streets because of my skin color. I don't know what it's like to be eyed with suspicion when I walk through a nice neighborhood. Though I live in Atlanta today, I'm from Connecticut, a world away from the racial segregation once found (and, truth be told, still found at times) in the South. I was just a teenager when King marched through Selma, only dimly aware of these epic civil rights clashes. I lived a world apart from the "colored only" drinking fountains, the segregated buses, the lynchings.

What could I possibly bring to the discussion?

I turned down the opportunity to speak. "I'm not the right person," I said.

But then, just a few days later, I found that one of my sons and his wife were about to adopt a little baby boy—part white, part African American.

They named him Jack. After me.

I thought about little Jack's future. *What world would he grow up in? What struggles would he face? Would he live in a nation that would at long last live up to Thomas Jefferson's lofty words—that all men are created equal?*

A week after I turned the group down, they called me again and asked if I would reconsider speaking at the racial reconciliation lunch. This time I said yes. I told the group that little Jack had helped me see that the story of the civil rights struggle isn't just black history; it's *our* history—a story that involves and impacts us all. And it's up to us—all of us—to make the world a little better. To reshape it in a way that reflects God's love and resembles his glorious kingdom.

And you know what the key is to that happy ending? Mercy.

Get Close Enough to Touch

We come back to the story of the Good Samaritan. Bishop Alexander, in his talk, brought up a point in the story that I think is pretty relevant. The priest and the Levite—the people who crossed to the other side of the street to avoid the half-dead man—only saw the beaten soul from a distance. Alexander thinks maybe the priest and the Levite never got close enough to see that the man was alive at all. They saw him, assumed he was dead, and walked on by.

But the Good Samaritan came close. He bent down. He saw the fresh wounds, heard the labored breathing, smelled the blood and dirt on the body. And he did something about it.

It's easy for people like me to look, from a distance, at the ongoing fight for equality and make snap judgments about what could and should be done. It's easy for all of us to look at the poor and homeless and say, "Well, they must be at fault." We can glance at people caught up in the judicial system and say, "They had it coming." We can observe the mentally or physically ill and walk, quickly, to the other side.

Things look better from a distance, don't they?

Too often in the church we keep the people we need to show mercy to at a distance. We outsource our compassion. We write our checks and put them in the offering plate. We send off our donations to faraway lands we'll never see and wouldn't want to. The closest we sometimes get to the people we try to help is through a picture. Or a video. Maybe a speaker or two. We try to heal from a distance.

But what did Jesus do? He *touched* those who needed healing. He saw their faces, heard their cries, and literally reached out and touched them. He put his fingers in a deaf man's ears (see Mark 7:33). He rubbed mud over a blind man's eyes (see John 9:6). When a soldier's twelve-year-old daughter died before Jesus could visit, the Son of God went in anyway. "Taking her by the hand he said to her, 'Talitha cumi,' which means 'Little girl, I say to you, arise'" (Mark 5:41).

Look at the stories of mercy we've covered in this chapter. The touch between Lola the slave and her dying master. Adriaan Vlok washing the feet of the man he had tried to kill. The Good Samaritan—the "do" part of his story—when he touched the traveler. He bandaged the man's wounds.

189

He poured oil and wine on them. He placed the man on his donkey. Human contact, intimate and real, is an essential part of the story.

Touch communicates a level of intimacy and commitment that a check will never do, no matter how big it is. When we're close enough to touch, we're close enough to see the problems and issues as they really are, not as we imagine them to be.

Jesus *touched*. Shouldn't we do the same?

Mercy, Even behind Bars

Pete Ochs is a successful Kansas businessman. He's been an investment banker and a CEO of several companies, and he loves Christ with all his heart.

A few years ago, Pete decided to hire convicts. Not former convicts but current ones locked up in the Hutchinson Correctional Facility. He moved some of his operations to the facility, working with criminals from every background. Some of them have been locked up for murder. A few may spend the rest of their lives behind those prison walls. But for Pete, the move was important. He didn't do it just because he needed cheap labor. He wanted to change a few lives.

By giving the prisoners work, Pete is giving them skills that might pay off outside of prison. He sponsors regular practical classes for his employees: how to be a better father, for instance, or how to manage your money. Pete even encourages charity inside the facility. If his employees donate some of their wages to any one of several nonprofit organizations on a list, Pete will match their contributions dollar for dollar.

The prisoners likely appreciate all these charitable efforts on their behalf. But you know what impresses them the most? That Pete doesn't give all this goodwill remotely. He and his wife, Deb, visit the facility regularly. They talk with their employees. Eat with them. Ask about their families and lives. They don't just *say* their prison-based employees are important to them; they prove it by actually spending time with them.

"Not too long ago, [Pete] was in our living area," a prisoner says in the video "Jailhouse Generosity."[21] "I've never seen a volunteer do anything like that. He's come to church with us. He's come to banquets that we've had. He's very involved and you can tell he's invested."

Invested. There's another word a businessman like me can resonate with.

When you invest in something financially, it means you're committed to the success of that thing. You do more than track the numbers; you root for it. You believe in it.

When you invest in people, it's the same thing. You can't be invested from a distance. You've got to be there. Seeing. Touching. Celebrating successes. Working through hardships.

This, my friends, is the essence of mercy.

The Divine View

Have you heard MercyMe's song "I Can Only Imagine"? If not, you might be one of the few who hasn't. The song became a phenomenon in 2001, selling millions of copies and landing on several music charts. Bart Millard wrote that song after his father died of cancer, imagining what his dad was experiencing in heaven.

But until recently, few people knew the rest of the story.

Millard's father, Arthur, was abusive. Sometimes Bart's dad beat him so badly that he could barely lie down. According to the 2018 film dramatization *I Can Only Imagine*, Arthur contracted cancer when Bart was a freshman in high school and, around the same time, had a life-changing encounter with Christ.

In the film, Arthur (played by Dennis Quaid) tries to make amends with his son (J. Michael Finley), asking him if he'd want to restore an old Jeep with him—just father and son doing something together, to make up for at least a part of the past.

But Bart's not interested; the wounds go too deep. Bart yells at his father and storms out of the house, making it perfectly clear just what he thinks of his dad's lame attempt at reconciliation.

But then Bart hears his father in a barn-turned-garage, smashing that Jeep—that symbol of hope for a rejuvenated father-son relationship—with a baseball bat.

Bart comes into the barn and sees his father on the ground, exhausted. Bart picks up the bat, clenching it so hard his knuckles turn white.

"Do it," Arthur says. *Do it*.

Bart wants to. You know he does.

But he drops the bat and offers a hand instead.

It proved to be a critical turning point for the father and son. "He went from the monster to the guy I wanted to be like when I grew up," Bart told Fox News in a 2014 interview. For about five years, until Arthur succumbed to his cancer, Arthur and Bart were "best friends."[22]

The only way to truly understand divine mercy is to understand that, in a way, we are all Arthur. We are Adriaan Vlok. We are Lola too. We sin. We hurt. We hunger for help. We thirst for mercy. We are both innocent and guilty, in need of a womb. We need a Good Samaritan to pick us up off the ground and carry us to safety.

God sees us. Hears our cries. He reaches down to touch us, to heal us.

But we have a hard time doing the same for others.

In the wake of the protests against police brutality in 2016, someone asked me, "Do all lives matter or do black lives matter?" I thought the question was absurd. Of course all lives matter.

But I've been given a new perspective since then. Today I see something different behind the Black Lives Matter movement. In those three words, we hear the pain of people. The distress. The shameful history.

"Can you just look at me?" it says. "Can you just listen to me right now? Can you just try, for a minute, to step into my shoes?"

Mercy looks . . . and sees. Mercy listens . . . and hears. Mercy touches . . . and feels. Divine mercy goes beyond what we feel in the moment, what we think might be practical. Sometimes God's impulse can be hard to follow. It's difficult to drop the bat when our anger and hurt and even logic suggest we should swing away.

The more challenging the impulse is to follow, the more transformative it can be. And perhaps if enough people have the courage to follow God's impulse, we could change the world.

God's Pattern of Love for You: Following Through

Bishop Alexander says the difficult and unjust history of racism in our country is not our fault but is our problem. We are called to go and serve those who are different from us. Pray about your relationships and ask God to open up doors for you to become friends with people who are different from you.

PART 4

ENDURE:
The Discipline of Mercy

SHOW PERSEVERANCE
AND DEDICATION

*"Take care of him," [said the Samaritan],
"and whatever more you spend, I will repay
you when I come back." (Luke 10:35)*

8

The Two Deals

The Good Samaritan parable covers thirteen verses in Luke 10, giving us a powerful, poignant story rich in meaning and resonance. But my favorite part of the parable is summed up in four simple words: "I will . . . come back" (v. 35).

In our steps to follow God's mercy, we *see*. We *go*. We *do*. And then . . . we *endure*.

The Good Samaritan endured. He knew the traveler's wounds wouldn't patch up overnight. As we talked about in chapter 6, he paid the innkeeper's room and board for as long as three weeks, promising to pay more if the bill was higher.

Mercy is about being faithful, both to the process and to the people involved. And being faithful requires time, perseverance, and dedication. To be faithful means we're in it for the long haul.

Jesus told us that "one who is faithful in a very little is also faithful in much" (Luke 16:10). In Proverbs 20:6, Solomon writes, "Lots of people claim to be loyal and loving, but where on earth can you find one?" (Message). Faithfulness is very important and very rare. And in the realm of faithfulness—as with all things merciful—we learn how to be faithful from God.

I love what 2 Timothy 2:12–13 says: "If we endure, we will also reign with him; if we deny him, he also will deny us; if we are faithless, he remains faithful—for he cannot deny himself."

God is perfectly faithful to us, his covenant people, even when we're not faithful to him. It's part of his very nature.

Hesed Love

Not many people, even in the Bible, see God. Moses is one of the few who came close to the Lord's physical presence. God caused his glory to pass by Moses, descending "in a cloud." And in that infinitely precious, infinitely rare moment, God introduced himself (Exod. 34:5–7). God proclaimed his name to Moses and described himself as "merciful and gracious, longsuffering, and abundant in goodness and truth" (v. 6 KJV).

This phrase is the translation for a single Hebrew word, *hesed*. It is a notoriously difficult term for translators to handle since it has no precise English equivalent, and it is variously translated as "loving-kindness," "mercy," "steadfast love," and "goodness."

But if we hope to understand God, it's a word we must seek to understand as well. *Hesed* appears some sixty-six times in the Old Testament alone, which suggests its importance.

Hesed love connotes covenant fidelity, steadfastness, and persistence—all characteristics that mark God's abiding love for his people. As scholar Norman Snaith describes, "God's loving-kindness is that sure love which will not let Israel go. Not all Israel's persistent waywardness could ever destroy it. Though Israel be faithless, yet God remains faithful still."[1] God's enduring allegiance to Israel is full of mercy because this hesed love of his is so often "one-way." God showers his love on his people, but so often we do not return it in kind.

This truth is worth lingering on for a bit. This faithful loving-kindness that pursues us even in the face of indifference, ingratitude, or rejection is truly otherworldly. It's supernatural. It's divine. This is the love God has shown to us in the gospel of our salvation. It's the generous love that cost Jesus his life.

Hesed love involves deep, personal commitment—even though that commitment typically narrows the giver's personal freedom.

Moreover, hesed love "lands." It's never abstract or neglects the people immediately present in our lives. It's committed to relationship—real, honest-to-goodness connection with those around us that goes well beyond a written check.

Even more stunningly, hesed love "does not look at the fairness of love; *its commitment has nothing to do with how the other person treats you.*"[2] Hesed, author Paul E. Miller explains, "loves regardless of the response. It does not demand recognition or equality. It is uneven."[3] Hesed is determined love, resolved to do good to another regardless of the cost.

Hesed is the nearly unbelievable, totally undeserved, and almost inconceivably generous love of God toward us—the love that reached its pinnacle in the cross of Jesus. Hesed is the love that compelled Jesus to Calvary; the motivation behind the atonement. When we truly behold this great love—when we intentionally meditate on it—it can change us. Taking in the breadth, depth, length, and width of God's generous love toward us, we begin to find power and motivation to love others. It's how we should—how, in the end, we want to—respond to that matchless generosity.

How Great a Salvation

It stuns me to think of God's enduring faithfulness toward us. He shows us mercy even—especially—when we don't deserve it. He endures our slights. He loves us always. He can't stop himself. In him we have a Creator, Redeemer, Sustainer, and Savior. He has given us so much. It's like the old hymn by Thomas Chisholm: "Great is Thy faithfulness. . . . Thy compassions, they fail not. As Thou hast been Thou forever wilt be."

As God asks us to be ever more like him, he asks us to look at his enduring faithfulness and show it to others. To be strong and enduring when the world is weak and fickle. To love when it'd be so much easier to hate. I can picture Jesus saying, "Be faithful even to the point of death, and I will give you the crown of life."

Sound difficult? You bet it is. I wonder if that's why, paradoxically, the church seems to expect so little from us. To ask us to do what God *really* asks of us feels audacious. Maybe even impossible. To ask of churchgoers what God asks of his children seems like a recipe to turn folks away. So churches keep things simple. Easy. Undemanding.

There's a well-known pastor who asks each of his church's members to give a small donation to a special campaign each year. Some of us spend more on coffee in a week. A church I love dearly asks its leaders to memorize two Scriptures— *two*—for a leadership exam: one on infant baptism and one on divorce.

Really? Are these the first portions of Scripture a leader in a church should know?

The Christian walk should be a transformative journey— something that shakes our lives and could shake the world. But many churches aren't even worried about doing much to shake up our days.

I love what Hebrews 2:3 says: "How shall we escape if we neglect such a great salvation?" We worship an almighty God who turned the universe upside down for us—who will wait and remain faithful through all eternity. Do the lost truly understand that every knee shall bow and every tongue confess that Jesus Christ is Lord? Does the world know that we cannot truly love until we have been truly loved? Does the church itself know that it cannot reflect God's goodness without a balance of mercy and truth?

"Great is Thy faithfulness," we sing. Can any of us fathom how great that faithfulness is? And as we set our steps to follow God in this way of mercy, do we understand how much is asked of us in return?

Have I Got a Deal for You

Our call to care isn't a new thing. Ever since God created us, he's invited us to participate in his business of bringing the kingdom to earth. A little like my former boss, the billionaire, he calls us to go out into the world and be his representative. God is a deal-making God, and he calls his deals "covenants."

The Hebrew word for covenant is *berith*, which means "to cut." In ancient times, when two parties reached an agreement, they would cut an animal in half and walk between the halves as a symbol of their agreement. It's from this ceremony that we get our modern phrase "Let's cut a deal."

God cut his first deal with Adam and Eve, and it was a good one: live in Eden for the rest of eternity in peace and joy and communion with the Creator. It doesn't get much better. But the deal fell through when Adam and Eve took a bite of something they shouldn't have. When they ate from the tree of the knowledge of good and evil, God knew they were taking in something he didn't design us for. When we see the chaos and addictions in the world today, it's clear that this "knowledge of evil" is still crippling us.

But despite that early disappointment, God wasn't done dealing. He made covenants with Abraham and Moses, with Jonah and David. Each deal God made became more favorable for us, even as it grew more costly for him.

But his covenants with us were initially based on works. He made massive promises to his servants if they followed him and his commandments—which, unfortunately, proved impossible for people to do. God's covenants were constantly being broken—not by God, but by us. Our own failings made it hard for us to partner with him.

God's Deal

My friend, Pastor Johnny Hunt, once said to me, "Today, people want to *define* the gospel more than they want to *live* the gospel." I agree with him. Perhaps that's because defining the gospel is relatively easy whereas living the gospel—particularly when it comes to this area of endurance—is more challenging.

As G. K. Chesterton famously writes in *What's Wrong with the World*, "The Christian ideal has not been tried and found wanting. It has been found difficult; and left untried."[4] When we make a deal with God, he doesn't settle for lukewarm commitment from us. Why should we go into a covenant with God with a halfhearted effort when he—the Creator of the universe—goes all in?

One of the first and most important deals he made happened way back in Genesis 12. It's called the Abrahamic covenant, and its core principles read like this:

> And I will make of you a great nation, and I will bless you and make your name great, so that you will be a blessing. I will bless those who bless you, and him who dishonors you I will curse, and in you all the families of the earth shall be blessed. (Gen. 12:2–3)

Now, that covenant is surely expired by now, right? I mean, God made that promise to Abraham thousands of years ago.

But according to Paul, that covenant peered into the future. "And the Scripture, foreseeing that God would justify the Gentiles by faith, preached the gospel beforehand to Abraham, saying, 'In you shall all the nations be blessed'" (Gal. 3:8).

This covenant lies at the heart of mercy, especially when it comes to enduring mercy. And when we miss the connection of Abraham's covenant to where we are today, we risk missing the whole point. And it gets back to how—in Johnny Hunt's words—we define the gospel.

Some people use a "thin" definition of what the gospel is—unpacked primarily in the Bible's four Gospels (Matthew, Mark, Luke, and John). These books are all about Jesus and reading them gives us the straightforward story of Jesus's sacrifice for us. How he died for our sins and that this "free gift"—not our own works—gives us the path to eternal life.

Then you've got the "thick" gospel that encompasses the Bible in its entirety, tracking the story of the world and its people from its creation, fall, redemption, and finally, restoration. When you take this thick view, Jesus's work on the cross becomes part—albeit a critical part—of the overall story. We get a sense that the story doesn't end with Jesus's crucifixion, death, and resurrection; it continues through us, as Jesus works through us to make all things new.

That's a big deal. We're part of God's good news. We're part of his hesed love. We—like people who lived thousands of years ago and people who might live thousands of years in the future—are a piece of God's loving covenant.

When we look at the thick gospel, we truly get a sense of scale for God's faithfulness. The book spans thousands of years, and throughout we see how God's chosen people sometimes broke his heart. He can be angry and exasperated. But his faithfulness endures. His mercies remain.

I like this thick gospel because we better see God's heart and purpose behind it all—to bless us.

It reminds me of a wedding I attended a few years ago. Much of the service was exactly as you'd expect it to be. The man said his vows. The woman said hers. We all know how weddings go, right? But when the woman finished her piece, she didn't wait for the pastor to say, "You may now kiss the bride." Instead, she *launched* herself into the groom for the sealing kiss—practically jumping into his arms.

Now, look at that Abrahamic covenant again. What repeats again and again? Not the words *I do*, as we'd hear at a wedding, but something pretty close to that: the words *I will*. God uses that phrase several times. I will. I will. I will. I will. It's emphatic, loving, eager. God is excited about this covenant, even though he surely knows he'll be far more faithful to us than we will be to him. When I hear those repetitions of *I will*, I picture our Groom ready to launch his body into us.

We should be equally excited. After all, it's the perfect deal for us. He has our backs. He'll bless those who bless us and curse those who curse us. Moreover, God wants us to bless "all the families of the earth" (Gen. 12:3). How beautiful is that?

But that very section of the covenant—where it talks about our blessing the world—is also a condition. A catch. As much as God promises to bless us, so we must return the favor and promise to bless others. It's so important that God says it twice: "I will bless those who bless you, and him who dishonors you I will curse, and in you all the families of the earth shall be blessed."

That's our role in this strange, wonderful relationship with God. If he gives to us, and we do not pass it on, the blessing stops.

It's important to reiterate that God *gives* us these blessings that he wants us to pass on to others. It's so easy to believe that our talents, wealth, or any of the other elements we "possess" are somehow products of our own doing. But

God makes it clear that all of it—everything we are and everything we own—ultimately stems from him. Look at what Paul writes in 1 Corinthians 4:7: "For who sees anything different in you? What do you have that you did not receive? If then you received it, why do you boast as if you did not receive it?"

Technically, when we give even of ourselves, we're regifters! And when we look at all the gifts we've been given—the brightly wrapped presents of our talents, time, and treasure—maybe we'll see a clue somewhere on the wrapping paper regarding to whom and where and when we should pass the gift (or a portion of it) on.

God's deal is set up so that we should always be asking God, "Do you want me to bless someone else with this?"

It's funny. I think that sometimes even in church we're encouraged to look at the world around us with selfish eyes. I've heard pastors asking for money say, "God and I want something for you, not something from you." But when you read the gospel—the thick one—we see a different message: it's not all about you.

That's a critical, countercultural message in today's selfish age. It's not all about us. Yes, God blesses us in countless ways. But he wants us to turn around and bless other people with those very same gifts. God doesn't tell us to hold off if it's hard or the road feels a little long. He wants us to bless the world. It's in the contract. It's in the covenant.

Humankind's Deal

We find a very different "deal" struck just one chapter before the Abrahamic covenant, in Genesis 11. The story goes as follows:

Now the whole earth had one language and the same words. And as people migrated from the east, they found a plain in the land of Shinar and settled there. And they said to one another, "Come, let us make bricks, and burn them thoroughly." And they had brick for stone, and bitumen for mortar. Then they said, "Come, let us build ourselves a city and a tower with its top in the heavens, and let us make a name for ourselves, lest we be dispersed over the face of the whole earth." (vv. 1–4)

These people were building, of course, the Tower of Babel. *Babel* in Hebrew means "gate of God," and it's pretty clear that its builders—Hamites, we're told, who were descendants of Noah's son Ham—were hoping to get closer to God, but on their terms. Instead of following a covenant of God's making, these people wanted to set their own conditions.

This is the essence of religion—setting our own terms in how we relate to God.

We excel at making our relationship with God exceedingly complicated—just like those who tried to build the Tower of Babel.

Today we hear the story of Babel and it seems so obviously foolish. After all, we know what's in the heavens. We know God doesn't live somewhere in space, just left of Jupiter. *How silly of those people to try to build a tower to God,* we think.

But what they did isn't so different from how we operate when trying to reach out to our own ideas of God. We too attempt to build our own way to God, even though the whole point of the gospel (the thin one) is that it's impossible to do so. We can't work our way to God; the Almighty must reach down to us.

207

Just look at all the other ways Babel's tower-builders mis-understood who God was—many of which feel pretty famil-iar to how we also misunderstand God:

- God wants people scattered all over the earth. The work-ers didn't want to be scattered.
- In the Abrahamic covenant in Genesis 12, God said he would make our name great. The builders wanted to make names for themselves.
- God's covenant with us is based on his promises—the "I wills" in the pact. The workers cut God out of their plans entirely, even as they tried to build a tower to him.
- Even in their selection of building materials, the build-ers seemed to forsake God's lead and follow their own. They specifically used brick (their own man-made build-ing materials) instead of stone (which God made). It's a telling detail in the story—a way to stress that in building this tower to God, they wouldn't rely on him one iota.

Obviously, Christianity doesn't seem to be quite so self-focused. Every branch of and denomination in our faith claims to focus on God, not humankind. And I believe that's meant sincerely.

But it's important to remember that religion itself is a man-made construct. God simply desires relationship with us. And while God wants the church to be an integral part of that relationship—indeed, it is a divinely appointed institution—sometimes our churches get lost in the weeds. We co-opt that relationship and turn it into systems of rules and theology so complex that the world is literally filled with sects, denominations, and theological offshoots. (Call yourself a Baptist? You might belong to one of sixty-two branches of Baptists in the United States alone. Unless, of course, you adhere to one of the seventeen state or inter-state branches that lies outside those national definitions.)[5] Some of those theological distinctions are, obviously, very important. But when I recall the violent schism between the Russian Orthodox Church and the Old Believers in the seventeenth century, precipitated largely as to whether one should use two fingers or three to make the sign of the cross, I wonder how much God really cares about some of those distinctions.

Look outside the church, and things get even worse. Even those who don't believe in God are trying to build a tower to their own gods, be they named materialism or pleasure or some sort of global utopia.

When we look at the goals of Babel's builders through the world's eyes, who they were and what they wanted to achieve, everything sounds so good. They had a common vision and a common language. They knew what they wanted to do and were wholly unified in their ambition. In my world, it might be the sort of language that you'd read on an annual report.

The spirit of Babel is the spirit of the age.

The Gift of Confusion

We all know what happened to the builders of Babel.

> And the LORD said, "Behold, they are one people, and they have all one language, and this is only the beginning of what they will do. And nothing that they propose to do will now be impossible for them. Come, let us go down and there

confuse their language, so that they may not understand one another's speech." (Gen. 11:6–7)

Have you ever noticed that when we start going in the wrong direction, we can be overtaken by confusion? God gave the people over to babel, which means "to confound or confuse" and is very similar to Babel. In that sense, confusion is a gift because it is an indication that we are not in sync with God's plans.

But too often—particularly when it comes to our relationship with God—we don't realize how confused we really are. Like the Hamites who built the Tower of Babel, we continue to try to push our way to him rather than following his covenants.

Yes, the people building the tower were productive and smart. But they weren't wise. They didn't understand God at all. So God set them right by knocking them back.

Just one chapter later, in comes Abraham and his covenant with God.

I find this particularly interesting, because we find in Abraham almost a mirror image of what we find in the Tower of Babel.

The builders of Babel thought they knew exactly where they were going—straight up to heaven—even though they really didn't know where they were going at all. The confusion came after.

In contrast, Abraham started out confused. "By faith Abraham obeyed when he was called to go out to a place that he was to receive as an inheritance. And he went out, not knowing where he was going" (Heb. 11:8). All he knew was that "he was looking forward to the city that has foundations, whose designer and builder is God" (v. 10).

The Hamites tried to build their own tower under their own power. "Let us," they said. The result was confusion and failure.

Abraham heard God's promises. "I will," God told him, and so Abraham followed, even though he didn't know exactly where he was going. The result was a multitude of nations.

The Oldest Bridge

Travel to Izmir, Turkey, and you will find a simple, arched bridge curling over the Meles River. It doesn't look like a particularly remarkable bridge. It's attractive enough and it functions as a bridge ought to do, allowing people and vehicles to pass from one side of the Meles to the other.

What's remarkable about it is its age. The Caravan Bridge, as it's called, was built in 850 BC, back when Izmir was known as Smyrna, future home to one of the seven churches mentioned in Revelation. It was built when the divided kingdoms of Judea and Israel still stood. It has weathered the reign of Greeks and Lydians, Romans and Ottomans. Every day for nearly the last three thousand years, the bridge has done its job without flash or fanfare. It's simply a bridge—the oldest recorded bridge in the world. And it shows no sign of being replaced.

God, moved by mercy, built a bridge for us. And we, in turn, must build bridges for others. Just like real bridges, our merciful bridges can look and feel and operate quite differently from one another, but they all have the same purpose: to get people from one place to another. Real bridges span rivers and channels and chasms. Our bridges of mercy cross the span over hurt and destruction, and they provide a way for those in need of mercy to get to a different, better place. They convey people from need to enough, from danger to safety, from hate to love.

Moreover, our mercy, because it's a reflection of God himself, also brings people closer to him.

But bridges are typically long-term structures, sometimes built over decades and used for centuries or millennia. Likewise, mercy is a process, and it can be a long, ongoing one. Just as each one of us is always in need of God's mercies, so people will be in need of ours—and sometimes for longer than we'd like.

Faithfulness

As we try to follow God ourselves on this journey of mercy, we're a little like Abraham. Most of our world doesn't know God and doesn't want to. It's filled with bluster, noise, and confusion, and it can be difficult to hear God's still, small voice through the babel.

Hopefully, the steps we've outlined in this book help us hear God a little better, understand God's impulse more clearly, and feel it beat in our own chests.

We must see the need of mercy, be it for a friend, a stranger, a starving untouchable widow halfway around the world, or an unlovable coworker in the cubicle next to you.

We must go—moving forcefully to that need to see where we can help.

And then we must do. We must bandage the wounds. Feed the hungry. Seek justice for the persecuted. Help. Hug. Love.

But as we've seen, that's not the end of the road with us. God understands how much we need his ongoing mercy.

And that's the posture we must assume with those whom we show mercy to as well. We must endure.

Yes, there are off-ramps. Yes, there are sometimes limits.

When I think about enduring mercy, I think of my friend and his son, Stephen.

Stephen is twenty-six. He's smart. Handsome. Talented. He has all the tools he needs to succeed in life.

But he doesn't have a job, and he hasn't had one for years. He suffers from depression, anxiety, and other mental health issues—problems the church often ignores. Sometimes he's too angry to speak. Or he'll burst into tears for no reason at all. He's talked about suicide. He's walked away from his Christian upbringing. No, sprinted is more like it. He believes Christians are the root of, not the solution to, this world's problems.

He's a prodigal in a way—lost and hurting. And like the prodigal son, he's coming back home—back to live with his Christian mother and father.

Stephen's father wants to show mercy to his son, following the process we've outlined. He saw the young man's desperate need. He went to him and asked him if he'd like to move back in. And now, he's in the process of doing—showing daily doses of mercy in the midst of Stephen's ups and downs. Patience. Love. Guidance. Maybe a little hope. With luck, being at home may help Stephen. But it might not. And no timeline exists for when he might be better. This process could take years or it might never end at all.

"It's not how I imagined parenthood would look like by now," he told me once. "It's not what I had hoped for him."

Sometimes it seems as though my friend is grieving—grieving for a little boy who's not really there anymore.

Yes, mercy is about seeing and going and doing, but maybe above all, it's about enduring.

We have no magic cures for the ills of this world. As much as I'd like to, I can't snap my fingers and free India's slaves or blink and cure this country's racial injustice. It takes more than a well-timed word or a generous check to save the hurting people I come across. It takes time. It takes commitment. It takes a willingness to engage with these people not just day after day but year after year, even when it seems like progress crawls like a snail or doesn't crawl at all.

The Samaritan summed up this fourth and final step of mercy with four words: "When I come back." Such deceptively beautiful, powerful words. He didn't assume the man would be healed. For the Samaritan, this wasn't a single good deed that was now completed and done. He saw that this demonstration of mercy was about more than just bandages and denarii. It was about a relationship.

When we get to this point, there are no more off-ramps. No excuses. We're in it for the duration.

Why? Because mercy is love made physical. Tangible. Touchable.

Because love believes all things, hopes all things, endures all things.

Because love never fails.

God's Pattern of Love for You: Enduring

Picture the three-thousand-year-old Caravan Bridge. We have discussed mercy as a bridge for others—a bridge that endures. Jesus said to the Smyrna church, "Be faithful, even to the point of death, and I will give you life as your victor's crown" (Rev. 2:10 NIV).

This crown of life is one of five crowns Jesus can bestow on us at the judgment.

Is there an area in your life or a relationship that you feel tempted to give up on now? Ask Jesus for strength. He will reward you for enduring.

9

The Covenant of Intimacy

God's goodness is his glory; and he will have
us to know him by the glory of his mercy
more than by the glory of his majesty.

—*Matthew Henry*

Little Jack

Truthfully, I wasn't expecting much from the court proceeding. I was sure it was an administrative hearing.

Little Jack's adoption was a special event for our family. For my son Kurt and his wife, Melissa, little Jack was an answer to prayer. But to the government, our little family was one of many who needed something from the state—a signature here, a stamp there. As far as the state of Texas (where Kurt and Melissa live) was concerned, I was sure that Jack's adoption was simply a rote formality. Sign a few papers, answer a couple of questions, and that'd be that—a quick in and out declaring that little Jack was now officially a member of Kurt and Melissa's family.

But when I walked into that paneled courtroom, my breath was taken away.

At least thirty stuffed animals sat across the front of the courtroom, fluffy and smiling. We sat down in the first row for just a bit before we heard "Alexander" called from the front of the court. The five of us—Kurt, Melissa, my wife and I, and of course, little Jack—walked up to the bench where the judge sat. He smiled down on us.

"How have things been the last couple of months?" the judge asked Kurt and Melissa, who, like most adoptive parents, had spent time raising and caring for Jack before the adoption became official. They said it had been great. The judge asked if little Jack was healthy. Kurt and Melissa said he was.

And then he asked the parents-to-be three additional questions:

Would they love Jack forever?

Would they care for him forever?

Would they be his mother and father forever?

I looked at little Jack as I heard Kurt and Melissa respond yes to each question. I thought of little Jack's rocky beginnings and how his life had mysteriously, miraculously intersected with ours.

I thought about how, for the last few years, I'd spend time shooting basketball free throws in the driveway, silently saying a prayer with each one. Many of those prayers were centered on my children and grandchildren—that God would provide and care for them. I shot thousands of free throws, wondering if God was listening, excited to see what he might do.

I thought of this when I spotted an agreement called "In the Interest of a Child" after the proceeding. I was emotional reading the provision directing the state to issue a new birth certificate. The initial one would be sealed—it could never be accessed again. The provision directed that the boy's new name was John Clifford Alexander—our little Jack. A new life, a new name, a new birth certificate, forever parents. What a miracle!

As I look in the big bluish-gray eyes of my namesake, I know he has no clue how God arranged all this. He has life and hope because of the courage of his birth mother, a twenty-one-year-old woman. Proof that God is able to take our imperfect actions and turn them into something beautiful. As Romans 8:28 says, "We know that for those who love God all things work together for good, for those who are called according to his purpose."

Do you believe this is what God wants to do with each person? According to 2 Peter 3:9, God "is longsuffering to us-ward, not willing that any should perish, but that all should come to repentance" (KJV). Peter, in his first letter, writes, "Once you were not a people, but now you are God's people; once you had not received mercy, but now you have received mercy" (1 Pet. 2:10).

It is through the mercy of God and the gracious gift of Jesus Christ that we come into the eternal covenant with God through the blood of Jesus.

Who Is God to You?

I was so surprised to see that judge surrounded by stuffed animals. When we picture judges, we imagine them as stern and strict, scowling over the bench with gavel in hand, ready to hand out judgment. The Bible tells us that Jesus will return as a judge one day. I think we sometimes picture him in much the same way: strict, zealous, maybe even cold.

We picture God in other ways too. We see him as a king, expecting and deserving praise and sacrifice. We're asked to think about him as a father too. Indeed, Jesus instructed us to see God as Father—not just *his* father, but *ours*, which is emphasized in the opening words of the Lord's Prayer: "Our Father, who art in heaven, hallowed be thy name . . ." But if you're like me, that image of God as a father doesn't necessarily soften our picture of him. Some of us grew up without a father or with a difficult one. Theologian Walter Brueggemann hints at those difficulties when he says that some see God as "a nurturing mother while some see him as a disciplining Father."[1]

But this lens through which we see God determines so much of how we view others and ourselves. If God is a stern judge or a tough father to us, it will impact how, and even if, we pray. For so many years, I would hear the word *God* and my mind would draw a literal blank. We are the image of who we believe God to be.

Pastor A. W. Tozer writes, "The most important thing about *ourselves* is the first thing we think of when we think of God."[2] If we think God is demanding, we will likely be demanding. If we think God is mean, we will be mean. If our God is legalistic, we will be religious or rebellious. When we miss his mercies, it disturbs us and wreaks havoc in our world.

But if we see God as merciful, as compassionate, as loving—well, that too changes everything. If we see him not as a strict father ready to scold and punish but as a loving dad who picks us up in his arms and carries us home, it changes the cadence of our lives. When we hold that image of God in our hearts, it heals our wounds and eases our fears. In the spirit of Chuck Swindoll, mercy is relief from the pressure of our fallen lives and culture. Rick Warren says, "In a mean world, our greatest witness is showing mercy."[3]

Love is like the fountain of God, and what flows out of it is mercy. In Alexander MacLaren's biblical commentary on Ephesians 2:4, he writes,

> For surely a love which takes into account the sin that cannot repel it, and so shapes itself into mercy, sparing and departing from the strict line of retribution and justice, is great. And surely a mercy which refuses to be provoked by seventy times seven transgressions in an hour, not to say a day, is rich. That mercy is wider than all humanity, deeper than all sin, was before all rebellion, and will last forever. And it is open for every soul of man to receive if he will.[4]

This is why the Matthew Henry quote I used at the start of this chapter is so consequential. When we see God through his mercy, we get to know him. We're given a glimpse into his unseen heart. We understand who he is. Theologians seem to want to tell us about God rather than how to know him. Of course, we do need to worship him for his whole catalog of virtues, to revere him as holy and just, to bow in gratitude for making us righteous through Jesus, and to marvel at his plan for good. But mercy is something else again. Mercy is, as John Gill writes, "a perfection of the divine nature,"[5] and when we see this, we are meant to be stunned. We experience the intimacy of our covenant with God. We picture his presence on the mercy seat of the ark of the covenant atop the commandments. We remember the miracles of Aaron's rod and the golden bowl of manna. We understand God doesn't just judge us—he *loves* us.

Mercy makes all the difference. And when we don't see that mercy in the heart of God, it can lead to some sad disconnections in our hearts and relationships.

God's Ownership and the Intimacy Model

Our misconceptions of God contribute to a lack of intimacy in our covenant with him. And that lack of intimacy leads to some well-intentioned but ultimately shortsighted efforts.

In 2010, Bill Gates and Warren Buffett started something called The Giving Pledge.[6] That year, 158 billionaires (or in the words of the organization's website, "those who would be if not for their giving") pledged to give at least half of their net worth to philanthropy. The roster has now grown to 170 of "the world's wealthiest individuals, couples and families" from twenty-one countries.[7]

We've seen a similar drive in the Christian community. The faith's "generosity movement" encourages believers to give sacrificially.

The main tenet of this generosity movement is that God owns everything. We are merely managers of what God has loaned to us—*stewards* is the religious word—and thus we need to manage those gifts wisely. It's meant to cause people to draw financial "finish lines" so they will give away more money.

All that is well and good and even true. I can give some assent to the theology that God owns everything. But the concept does some damage to our relationship with God.

The Giving Pledge and the corresponding Christian generosity movement have done some good. But if our giving is centered on our wallets, then we are missing a far more intimate expression of generosity. For six years, I have been involved through The Reimagine Group to pivot these generous and worthwhile efforts toward holistic and relational generosity, not just financial. But most of the time, doing so has felt like walking out into surf in bad weather.

But I believe God wants more from us than just our money, no matter how many digits make up our bank accounts. He wants us to feel the same sort of love for his creation that he himself does. He wants us to enter into people's lives and relate to them.

And frankly, I don't think God cares all that much about what belongs to whom. He's far more concerned with what and whom we care about—how we relate to his gifts and his creation.

Think about how intimate that creation is from cradle to grave.

- *Procreation.* God wants to populate the earth, but how did he design us to make that happen? Through loving relationships and genetics intended to implant some of ourselves into the sons and daughters who come after us. Consider: The average man generates more than five billion sperm in his lifetime. Yet God, in his sovereignty, chooses our specific offspring. We see our children mirror some of our traits, and we experience joy through this. Is that child ours? Or God's?

- *Identity*. We are told that we are a child of God but that our "life is hidden with Christ in God" (Col. 3:3).

- *Life*. Galatians 2:20 says we have been crucified with Christ and "it is no longer I who live, but Christ who lives in me." Imagine the intimacy of our Savior taking on our whole catalog of sin and selfishness and becoming a sacrifice for *us*. When we review the world's ten thousand religions, nearly all require sacrifices to a god. Christianity is the only faith in which God makes himself a sacrifice for his followers. What a mercy!

- *Scripture*. Imagine choosing someone to tell your story. You would undoubtedly choose someone who thought well of you and was of strong character. God chose forty people over fifteen hundred years to tell his story—murderers, liars, immoral people, unfaithful people. He used their voices and their errors to display God's redemptive power and plan—his mercy. The sheer span of time in which he spoke through people is a picture of enduring mercy.

- *Our being*. Imagine the Holy Spirit of God taking residence in the souls of believers to comfort, lead, teach, and convict stubborn people of sin. Religion tries to change us from the outside; the Spirit of God changes us from the inside.

All this is so intimate and relational. It seems as though God does everything possible to not only give us identity but also infuse his life in ours. In many ways, it's like a marriage. There's a rhythm, a dance to the relational interplay between the parties. I often say that when a couple starts talking about who owns what, then they're probably on the brink of divorce. God gives us all things but asks us to consecrate them back to him for his purposes and glory. This is quite different from us being a manager like a stockbroker!

A Covenant of Salt

In the Old Testament, people made plenty of sacrifices to God, giving him everything from cattle to doves. But people didn't just sacrifice the animals. Every Old Testament sacrifice was accompanied by salt.

We sometimes disparage salt in these health-and-heart-conscious days. Many of us try to eliminate as much salt from our diets as possible. But even so, we need salt. And back in Jesus's day, salt was a treasured, near-miraculous commodity. It was so important that in Matthew 5 Jesus told us his followers were to *be* salt.

While it's well known that salt is a preservative and it brings out the flavor in food, I had no idea how necessary salt is to the human body and to life itself.

- Salt speeds up healing. We've all heard how painful it is to rub salt in a wound. But for thousands of years, people have tended to their wounds using saltwater. Indeed, saltwater is still used to disinfect wounds (it kills some problematic bacteria) and speed the healing process (it helps dry water and other liquid discharges around the wound).[8]
- Salt helps transmit nerve impulses around the body—so much so that, according to the Salt Association, our

225

nerves wouldn't function without it.[9] It's a remarkable regulating agent too, facilitating just the right fluid content in and around blood cells. Indeed, when someone's suffering from heart failure or horrific diarrhea or something else that makes it impossible to drink fluids, doctors will give them an intravenous saline solution to ensure the body's fluids get back to normal.[10]

- Salt not only enhances the flavor of food, but it actually helps facilitate our abilities to smell, taste, and even touch.[11]
- Salt is critical for our muscles to work correctly, including our biggest muscle, the heart. In fact, consuming salt is sometimes used to treat low blood pressure.

Salt impacts practically every system in our bodies, and it's used to treat everything from sore muscles to cystic fibrosis.[12] No wonder Jesus asked us to be like salt.

Jesus was telling us how radically important his followers are to the functioning of the whole world. We are to help transmit the taste, smell, and tactile functions of God! We are essential for healthy movement and relationships. We are meant to be agents of healing.

That healing is illustrated powerfully in a little-told tale in the Bible.

Tucked away in the pages of the Old Testament, we find the story of Elisha and the healing waters at Jericho—the same famous city that Joshua and his followers marched around, bringing its walls tumbling down. After the city fell, Joshua literally cursed it (see Josh. 6:26).

Hundreds of years after Joshua, Jericho—located at a strategic location west of the Jordan River—had been rebuilt. But all those new buildings didn't erase Joshua's ancient curse. The city's water supply was bad—so polluted, in fact, that it was poisoning everything it touched, including animals, people, and especially the land itself.

A problem that big demands a special solution, so the elders from Jericho found the biggest problem-solver around: Elisha, the famous prophet who was just beginning his own ministry, which he had taken over from Elijah. They brought him back to town and, according to 2 Kings 2:19–22, here's what happened next:

> The people of the city said to Elisha, "Look, our lord, this town is well situated, as you can see, but the water is bad and the land is unproductive." "Bring me a new bowl," he said, "and put salt in it." So they brought it to him. Then he went out to the spring and threw the salt into it, saying, "This is what the LORD says: 'I have healed this water. Never again will it cause death or make the land unproductive.'" And the water has remained pure to this day, according to the word Elisha had spoken. (NIV)

The story is short but fascinating. Before Elisha came to town in those ancient days, Jericho was probably known to most folks as a cursed city—a curse enacted by one of the Bible's most famous heroes and backed up by God himself.

But then Elisha came by, threw salt in a spring, and the water was restored. When that salt hit the water, it *dissolved*. It disappeared into the thing it was cleansing and purifying and flavoring. We might even say it "lost its life" for the sake of the water's healing. When Elisha tossed salt into Jericho's spring, he wasn't able to scoop it back out and use it again. It disappeared—used in the way it was intended. For the salt to do its work, it must dissolve, giving its life for the betterment of others. That which had brought only barrenness and grief became a source of life and fruitfulness.

The laying down of our lives—the dissolution of *our* salt—is what the gospel's all about. According to 1 John 3:16, "By this we know love, that [Jesus] laid down his life for us, and we ought to lay down our lives for the brothers."

The salt was a healing agent for the water of Jericho, dissolving in it and bringing life. Are we that same type of healing agent for the world? How willing are we to let our lives dissolve for the restoration of others?

A Low-Salt Faith and Mad Pigs

Here's an interesting sidenote for the covenant of salt. While God told his followers to always include salt with their sacrifices, he also told them to never, *ever* use honey.

That too seems strange to our modern ears. Honey's so sweet, after all. So tasty. Back then, in the days before processed sugar and corn syrup, it would've been the most effective sweetener around. Why not add it to make the offering even more pleasing?

But here's the thing: sacrifices were burned on altars. And honey, as sweet as it is, spoils in heat.

And yet I think that's just what many churches are offering God today: honey. The sweet sound of high-production worship music. The meaningless platitudes of a feel-good sermon. The offerings we stick in the plate—money we can do without, money we don't even know where it goes. We're all about being sweet these days. "Let's bundle church in the sweetest, most inoffensive package we can," we say. "That'll make Christianity seem relevant."

And so we spoil in the heat, adding nothing to the hurting world. In fact, we might even stink up the joint.

If Elisha tossed honey into the poisoned water, the water would still be poisoned—just sweeter. Honey is faith that makes us *feel* good, but it doesn't actually *do* good.

Because God wrote his law on the minds and hearts of human beings, we know on some level the role Christians have in bringing function and healing. Jesus didn't just call us the "salt of the earth" and leave it at that. He offered a stern warning. "You are the salt of the earth. But if the salt loses its saltiness, how can it be made salty again? It is no longer good for anything, except to be thrown out and trampled underfoot" (Matt. 5:13 NIV).

This same word, *trampled*, is used two chapters later with respect to not casting "pearls before pigs" (Matt. 7:6). My friend Darryl Ford researched this and believes the verse refers to "seed pearls," which look like seed but are actually hard and have no value as food. Throwing these "pearls" may cause the pigs to "trample them underfoot and turn to attack you" (v. 6). Pigs have no use for seed pearls—they want real food. If our role is to provide truth (food) and mercy (healing), and we don't provide it, should we be that surprised when this broken world—in need of food and healing—turns on us?

The Christian church wrings its hands over its fading influence. Christians fume over the disrespect the church is shown in the culture today and sometimes mistake this as persecution.

But is it persecution? Or is it the result of not being what Christ called us to be? Have we forgotten what it's like to be salt to a hungry, hurting world? Have we forgotten what it means to show mercy to people who desperately need God?

I wonder. I wonder whether, in our preoccupation to make Christianity as sweet as possible, we've lost the essence of Christ. We've lost that sense of ourselves—who we should be, who the world needs us to be.

I wonder whether our "persecution" is really a sign we've been thrown out. Whether we're being justly trampled. The dying world needs the salt of mercy in our sacrifices and the substance and nutrition in our truth messaging.

Truth and Justice

Most of us have at least a passing familiarity with the story of the ark of the covenant. Maybe we know it mostly from that old Indiana Jones movie *Raiders of the Lost Ark*—the fabled Jewish treasure that Indy and the Nazis were in a race to acquire (and an object so powerful it literally melted the faces off a few folks). Those of us familiar with the Old Testament know that it's a precious vessel built to hold, among other precious objects, the tablets on which God inscribed the Ten Commandments. The vessel—essentially a big box—was capped with an elaborate lid adorned with two angels, their wings bent toward each other. This angelic lid was called "the mercy seat."

Our God is a God of mercy and truth. I've said so repeatedly in this book. I've focused on mercy as the trait that motivated God to rescue us and the trait he expects to motivate us to sacrifice ourselves for others. Yes, as we discussed in the introduction, truth is the other "rail" that God's operating system runs on. But there is a reason why God's mercy seat sat on top of the commandments in the ark of the covenant.

Truth must be marinated in mercy. Surrounded by it. Covered by it.

Mercy is our womb. Our arms. Our sacred space in which truth can be both protected and manifested. Truth is foundational to our lives, but that truth works best in tandem with mercy. Those two critical aspects of God's character give us the two lenses through which to approach our faith and a broken world.

Some might balk at that. They say, "Wait a minute, truth is the revelation of God himself. He reveals his heart and his wisdom through truth." But James comes along and says that the wisdom from above is full of mercy and good fruits (see James 3:17). Mercy and truth must be in balance. We've seen what happens when that balance is lost—when we lean too much on one or the other. We see it all around us. And we've read about it in this book. When mercy is underrepresented and undertaught in the church, truth becomes a blunt, even cruel object.

Lightning and Thunder

As a child, I remember thunderstorms rumbling over our Connecticut home. I'd watch the lightning flash, listen to the thunder boom. And like most children, I'd be afraid. I could sense the power in those storms and understood some strange connection between the lightning and thunder. But only later in life did I learn that lightning actually precedes thunder.

Lightning is exceptionally hot and can reach temperatures as high as 54,000 degrees Fahrenheit.[13] It's so hot that, when lightning hits the air, the heat causes the air to essentially explode because it expands so quickly. This expansion causes the loud cracking noise and a roll of thunder.[14]

I think mercy and grace are meant to work in tandem, just as lightning and thunder do. We repeatedly see in Scripture that mercy is God's first impulse toward us, and in the parable of the Good Samaritan, it is the first impulse shown by the Samaritan to the beaten man.

"God's mere mercy . . . is the original source and moving cause of our salvation," writes the Reverend Joseph Benson in his commentary *The New Testament of Our Lord and Savior Jesus Christ*, "and by the enlightening, quickening, and renewing influences of the Holy Spirit, the efficient cause of it."[15]

When we show mercy to the poor, broken, and distressed and extend forgiveness from the heart to fellow sinners and our enemies, these expressions of mercy create positive "heat." When we reckon the value of a soul as greater than our schedules, resources, priorities, and pride, we are acting in God's impulse of mercy. In doing so, this heat of mercy provides a vacuum for the Spirit of grace to fill, like a roll of thunder. Just as God's "indescribable gift" in Christ was God's thunder following his mercy, we need to rethink the "lightning" of mercy in our lives.

Dietrich Bonhoeffer, among others, pointed out that grace, being free, often leads us to vertical gratitude and worship but not to the "expensive" love for our neighbor. The kind of love that costs us. In *The Cost of Discipleship*, he writes:

> The essence of grace, we suppose, is that the account has been paid in advance; and, because it has been paid, everything

can be had for nothing. . . . Cheap grace means grace as a doctrine, a principle, a system. It means forgiveness of sins proclaimed as a general truth, the love of God taught as the Christian conception of God. . . . Cheap grace therefore amounts to a denial of the Living Word of God.[16]

Grace *is* amazing, but mercy is not mere pity—it is magnificent! It is the heart of the Father. Grace will not only abound but also result in rolls of thunder as we unleash our lightning bolts of mercy!

Bridging

In the middle of writing this book, I sat through a series of church theology classes. We talked about characteristics of God that we could all imitate and experience from one another. Then we got into the "omnis" and holiness and sovereignty—traits of God that are wholly his and make him the one true God.

We didn't talk about mercy at all, which seemed curious to me. The most any other trait of God is listed in a row is three (e.g., holy, holy, holy). And yet in Psalm 136, we read "his mercy endures forever" (GW) twenty-six times; in Psalm 103, God's mercies are mentioned another five times (NKJV).

Yes, we should praise God for his majesty and perfect justice and amazing ways and plans. We may, and should, marvel at his ability to take ashes, often our ashes, and turn them into something beautiful. But we get to know him, *really* know him, through his mercy.

You're probably familiar with that famous illustration of a cross stretched across a chasm, bridging the span between

God's holiness and humankind's sinfulness. Likewise, in a bankrupt company, an advocate or heroic capital partner is needed to recapitalize, reorganize, and assume certain debts of the troubled entity.

As Christians, we are called to be a bridge too: a bridge to the poor, the distressed, fellow sinners, and enemies. We span the chasm between a hurting world and a healing God, allowing one to connect with the other.

In the introduction, we cited Jesus in his earthly ministry as forming that bridge composed of three components: mercy, truth, and relationship. This allows intimacy between us and those we love and serve. It's critical to understand that building bridges for others is a process, not just a deed or a gift, and that God can redirect us to relational off-ramps. This book is not a handbook on codependency and enabling.

But sometimes the bridge lasts a long time. Longer than anyone might have anticipated.

About eighteen years ago, my wife and I met Sherri. Her husband had left her, leaving her with a four-year-old son and an eighteen-month-old daughter. We befriended her and for fifteen years many Friday nights were Sherri nights. We'd share a meal together, and she'd talk about her week. Oftentimes she'd talk about the everyday needs she had. Maybe she was stretched thin, trying to meet practical and emotional needs. She'd talk about relational issues or the struggles of raising two children as a single parent. She'd share with us the intimacies of life, and we'd share ours with her. At the end of our evenings, we'd always pray together. We became very good friends. We were showing mercy, I suppose, but it wasn't a monetary thing; it was about relationship. Friendship. Sometimes we would help her, and sometimes she would help us.

A few years ago, we had the privilege of setting her up on a date with the man who is now her husband, and that friendship has grown to include him too. We were lucky enough to be a bridge for Sherri. And over our lifetimes, we've been a bridge to other people as well—the boys and young men I've mentored, the people we've connected with in ministry, the Indian untouchables half a world away. And sometimes we've been *given* a bridge. We've been shown mercy. That's what God's impulse is about. You show mercy. You give mercy. And those whom you've shown mercy to will, in turn, be more merciful to others.

God built a bridge for us—a covenant that is crossed through works. But the bridge was hard for us—too long, too perfect. We covered it with our sin, coated it with our guilt, and made it impassable.

And so God built us a new bridge—a bridge built on mercy and held by grace. He stands on the other side, arms open, eyes smiling. He bids us to come across by the cross, where he'll take our hands and lead us home.

Through the intimacy we experience with him, we are transformed. And from there, he'll send us out again—as his merciful emissaries, his servants, his partners. As I shared early on, when we are a womb, we shape others and are shaped ourselves.

God's Pattern of Love for You: Bridging

Is there an area of your life where you need mercy? According to Jesus, "Blessed are the merciful, for they shall receive mercy." Think of one person you can pray for or forgive or reach out to in kindness; then see what the Lord does for you.

Conclusion

GASP!

*H*ave you ever made someone gasp? I must warn you—
it is addictive.

Earlier, I recounted the scene from *Les Misérables* when
the bishop tells the police that Jean Valjean had "forgotten"
the candlesticks after Valjean repaid the bishop for his kindness by stealing the silverware. I gasped, just as the rest of
the audience gasped. I gasped again when he said to Jean
Valjean, "Tonight, I have bought your soul for God!"

Do we really understand that God is literally allowing us
to "play God" when we extend mercy? Unfortunately, you
and I rarely experience mercy from others. My friend is still
haunted by being upbraided by his father when he told him
that he had gotten his girlfriend pregnant. I was terrified in
court at age sixteen after I had hit another car's bumper while
on a steep hill; my mother ripped into me about how humili-
ated she was. We all have stories about when we needed the
hug but got slugged. The word that is missing in our world
is *tenderness*. Mercy expressed in tenderness—at the exact

time when justice is justified—is the heartbeat of this book. With attention spans of eight seconds, we aren't able to follow the Samaritan as he sees, goes, does, and endures. Our souls and the soul of our world are crying out for something more, only to be disappointed.

My friends who are in Alcoholics Anonymous will sadly say that they get more hugs and fellowship in their AA meetings than at church. I have spoken a number of times at an African American church in north Atlanta. After I addressed the church the first time, no less than fifty people hugged me. When I left, I gasped.

If you are a truth/doctrine person, I implore you to give mercy a "promotion." Psalm 25:10 says, "All the paths of the LORD are mercy and truth" (KJV). Jesus implores us to "be merciful, even as your Father is merciful" (Luke 6:36). Without mercy, it is all too easy to become modern-day pharisees. Meditate on what we have covered:

- Mercy was the first attribute that God shared with Moses to describe himself.
- Mercy is the first response of the Samaritan in the four-step pattern of love.
- God says he desires mercy more than sacrifice.
- God says mercy triumphs over judgment.
- God says to do justice but to love mercy.
- The presence of God was located in the mercy seat of the ark of the covenant, which sat *on top of* the commandments.
- God says we get a payback; in the Beatitudes, Jesus says, "Blessed are the merciful, for they shall receive mercy" (Matt. 5:7).

God shows us his heart, his life, his priorities in his blessed Word. James tells us that the Word is also a mirror in which we see our own hearts and lives (see James 1:22–23). What do you see? Are you willing to imitate the God Impulse of mercy modeled by the Father and the Samaritan? When was the last time you made someone gasp?

If you love people but have moderate or no regard for God's Word, I want to hug you! Perhaps you have been hurt, judged, or unlovingly disciplined by the "truth folks," and you have written off God in the process.

When I was in college, I hitchhiked from North Carolina to come home to see my mother and stepfather in Connecticut. I had told them I was coming. When I walked in the kitchen door after seventeen hours of hitchhiking, my stepfather walked past me and did not say a word. He had his car packed up and he left. I was *so* hurt. It was a reverse homecoming—he was not a father who ran to me but who drove away. I did not know what to do. It took me years to realize his pain. He knew my mother loved me more than him. After I became a Christian, I asked if he would be the best man in my wedding. I had gotten to a point where my desire to see healing in his life was greater than the pain in my own. It is so hard to get over pain.

You and I can never do it without the love of our real Father, our heavenly Father. He wants you to know him as the God who will run to a returning prodigal; the God who chose prostitutes, murderers, and adulterers for Jesus's bloodline; the God who, like the Samaritan, risked his life for a beaten enemy. And, finally, the God who sacrificed his precious blood on a cross for you and me. Each of us is like the two thieves who were on Jesus's side—one criticized Jesus, the other asked that Jesus remember him. We can't truly love God without knowing him; his Word is truth and our means of truly experiencing him and finding salvation that is only found in one Name. Find it in your heart to forgive the truth folks—it will make them gasp.

My favorite verses in the Bible show me God's heart for when I am reunited with him in glory. Hebrews 12:2 says, "For the joy set before him he endured the cross, scorning its shame, and sat down at the right hand of the throne of God" (NIV). Jesus endured for the "joy" set before him. The joy is us! It's you and me. Also, I had always thought God owned everything, but he is in our will, "the hope to which he has called you, the riches of his glorious inheritance in his holy people" (Eph. 1:18 NIV). He views our redemption as a blessed inheritance for him. Finally, according to Psalm 85:10, when "mercy and truth are met together; righteousness and peace have kissed each other" (KJV).

Allowing our truth to marinate in mercy, allowing mercy and truth to integrate ignites unity and, of all things, a kiss.

Go on the journey. Start with the God Impulse. Don't outsource your compassion.

Look at your life and ask God to show you people you can build a bridge for. How about that boy who just lost his dad? How about the nineteen-year-old whose mother left and whose dad is addicted to meth? How about the widow you can share your Friday nights with? How about that empty bedroom you can allow a single person to live in? The secret of life is that we will receive *our* healing and satisfaction as we bridge others.

SEE, GO, DO, ENDURE, then watch for the kisses—and listen for the gasps!

Notes

Introduction: Do We Bring Hope and Healing?

1. Peggy Noonan, "A Pope and a President in Poland," *Wall Street Journal*, July 6, 2017, http://www.peggynoonan.com/a-pope-and-a-president-in-poland/.

2. John Paul II, "Apostolic Journey to Poland Holy Mass Homily of His Holiness John Paul II," June 2, 1979, Victory Square, Warsaw, Poland, transcript, https://w2.vatican.va/content/john-paul-ii/en/homilies/1979/documents/hf_jp-ii_hom_19790602_polonia-varsavia.html.

3. Noonan, "A Pope and a President in Poland."

4. David Kinnaman and Gabe Lyons, *UnChristian: What a New Generation Really Thinks about Christianity . . . and Why It Matters* (Grand Rapids: Baker Books, 2007), 27–28, 34, 135.

5. David Kinnaman, "The Irrelevance of Faith," March 6, 2016, video, https://www.youtube.com/watch?time_continue=37&v=DCZ-t0qovOg.

6. Peggy Noonan, "People Are Afraid of Change," *Wall Street Journal*, November 9, 2012, https://www.wsj.com/articles/SB10001424127887323894704578107460045098692; Peggy Noonan, "What Comes after the Uprising," *Wall Street Journal*, November 11, 2016, https://www.wsj.com/articles/what-comes-after-the-uprising-1478824753.

7. Pope Francis, *The Name of God Is Mercy* (New York: Random House, 2016), 62.

8. "Induced Abortion Worldwide," Guttmacher Institute, September 2017, https://www.guttmacher.org/fact-sheet/induced-abortion-worldwide.

9. "Christian High School Bars Pregnant Teen from Graduation Ceremony," CBS News, May 24, 2017, https://www.cbsnews.com/news/christian-high-school-bars-pregnant-teen-from-graduation-ceremony/.

10. Jessica Chasmar, "Pregnant Teen Banned from Christian High School's Graduation for Being 'Immoral,'" *Washington Times*, May 25, 2017, http://www.washingtontimes.com/news/2017/may/25/maddi-runkles-pregnant-teen-banned

-from-christian-/?utm_campaign=shareaholic&utm_medium=email_this&utm
_source=email.

11. Chasmar, "Pregnant Teen Banned."

12. Kathryn Jean Lopez, "Support Life in the Mess of Human Life," *National Review*, June 19, 2017, http://www.nationalreview.com/article/448745/maddi-runk les-pregnant-christian-teen-celebrates-graduation.

Chapter 1 The God Impulse

1. "From Jerusalem to Jericho," American Bible Society, accessed November 9, 2017, http://bibleresources.americanbible.org/resource/from-jerusalem-to-jericho.

2. "Documents: 3 April 1968, I've Been to the Mountaintop, Memphis, Tenn.," Martin Luther King Jr. and the Global Struggle, accessed November 8, 2017, http://kingencyclopedia.stanford.edu/encyclopedia/documentsentry/ive_been _to_the_mountaintop/.

3. Pat McCloskey, "Why the Hatred between the Jews and Samaritans?" Franciscan Media, accessed November 9, 2017, https://www.franciscanmedia.org/the -rift-between-jews-and-samaritans/.

4. Tim Keller, *Ministries of Mercy: The Call of the Jericho Road* (Phillipsburg, NJ: P&R, 1997), 46.

5. "The Most Litigious Countries in the World," Clements Worldwise, accessed November 8, 2017, https://www.clements.com/resources/articles/The-Most-Liti gious-Countries-in-the-World.

6. Catherine Wynne, "The Teenager Who Saved a Man with an SS Tattoo," October 29, 2003, BBC News, http://www.bbc.com/news/magazine-24653643.

7. Wynne, "Teenager Who Saved a Man."

8. Wynne.

9. Wynne.

10. Martin Slagter, "Former Ann Arbor Resident Reflects on Saving Man from Beating at KKK Rally," Mlive, June 24, 2016, http://www.mlive.com/news/ann -arbor/index.ssf/2016/06/saving_man_from_beating_at_kkk.html.

11. Wynne, "Teenager Who Saved a Man."

12. Anne Lamott, *Hallelujah Anyway: Rediscovering Mercy* (New York: Riverhead Books, 2017), 8.

Chapter 2 Eight Seconds to See

1. Kevin McSpadden, "You Now Have a Shorter Attention Span than a Goldfish," *Time*, May 14, 2015, http://time.com/3858309/attention-spans-goldfish/.

2. McSpadden, "Shorter Attention Span."

3. "What Animal Has the Shortest Attention Span?" Reference.com, accessed November 13, 2017, https://www.reference.com/science/animal-shortest-attention -span-1eb06417bbb42012#.

4. YouTube Insights Team, "The First Five Seconds: Creating YouTube Ads That Break Through in a Skippable World," ThinkwithGoogle.com, June 2015, https://www.thinkwithgoogle.com/consumer-insights/creating-youtube-ads-that -break-through-in-a-skippable-world/.

5. David Kocieniewski and Gary Gately, "Man Shoots Eleven, Killing Five Girls, in Amish School," *New York Times*, October 3, 2006, http://www.nytimes.com/2006/10/03/us/03amish.html.

6. Jeff Glor, "Mother of Amish School Shooter Shares Amazing Story of Forgiveness," CBS News, December 12, 2013, http://www.cbsnews.com/news/mother-of-amish-school-shooter-shares-amazing-story-of-forgiveness/.

7. Timothy C. Morgan, "Purpose Driven in Rwanda," *Christianity Today*, September 23, 2005, http://www.christianitytoday.com/ct/2005/october/17.32.html.

8. Morgan, "Purpose Driven."

9. Michelle A. Vu, "Kay Warren on HIV/AIDS: God Broke My Heart, Wiped Me Out," *Christian Post*, December 1, 2010, http://www.christianpost.com/news/kay-warren-on-hiv-aids-god-broke-my-heartwiped-me-out-47890/.

10. Vu, "Kay Warren."

11. Vu.

12. Donald B. Kraybill, *The Upside-Down Kingdom* (Scottdale, PA: Herald Press, 1978).

13. Dr. Anna O'Brien, "Goats Are from Mars, Sheep Are from Venus," PetMD, September 13, 2013, http://www.petmd.com/blogs/thedailyvet/aobrien/2013/sept/goats-are-from-mars-sheep-are-from-venus-30886#.

14. "Matthew 13:15," *John Gill's Exposition of the Bible*, accessed November 13, 2017, http://www.biblestudytools.com/commentaries/gills-exposition-of-the-bible/matthew-13-15.html.

15. "What Is MS?" National Multiple Sclerosis Society, accessed November 13, 3017, http://www.nationalmssociety.org/What-is-MS.

16. Natalie Walters, "Playing These Six Video Games Could Help Improve Your Problem-Solving Skills," Business Insider, November 18, 2015, http://www.businessinsider.com/video-games-that-help-improve-problem-solving-skills-2015-10; "Action Video Games May Improve Hand-Eye Coordination," iLs Australia, accessed November 13, 2017, http://integratedlistening.com.au/blog/2014/10/21/action-video-games-may-improve-hand-eye-coordination/; Brian Handwerk, "Video Games Improve Vision, Study Says," National Geographic News, March 29, 2009, http://news.nationalgeographic.com/news/2009/03/090329-video-game-vision.html.

17. Matthew Grizzard, "Repeated Play Reduces Video Games' Ability to Elicit Guilt: Evidence from a Longitudinal Experiment," Taylor and Francis Online, March 30, 2016, http://www.tandfonline.com/doi/full/10.1080/15213269.2016.1142382.

18. Katie Rogers, "What Is a Constant Cycle of Violent News Doing to Us?" *New York Times*, July 15, 2016, https://www.nytimes.com/2016/07/16/health/what-is-a-constant-cycle-of-violent-news-doing-to-us.html?_r=0.

19. David Pogue, "Use It Better: The Worst Tech Predictions of All Time," January 18, 2012, https://www.scientificamerican.com/article/pogue-all-time-worst-tech-predictions/.

20. Jeremy Grantham, "Investing When Terrified," GMO, March 2009, http://ritholtz.com/wp-content/uploads/2009/03/jeremy-grantham-article-031009.pdf.

21. Melinda Wenner, " Smile! It Could Make You Happier," *Scientific American*, September 1, 2009, https://www.scientificamerican.com/article/smile-it-could-make-you-happier/.

22. Lynne Hybels, "A Common Friend to Arabs and Jews," *Lynne Hybels* (blog), November 28, 2011, https://www.lynnehybels.com/a-common-friend-to-arabs-and-jews/.

23. Hybels, "A Common Friend."

24. Lynne Hybels, "The Israeli-Palestinian Conflict: Six Things I Believe," *Lynne Hybels* (blog), December 8, 2013, https://www.lynnehybels.com/the-israeli-palestinian-conflict-six-things-i-believe/.

Chapter 3 The Womb

1. John Fricke and Phil Gast, "Police: Michigan Woman Gives Birth After Being Set on Fire, Shot," CNN, May 29, 2012, http://www.cnn.com/2012/05/29/justice/michigan-pregnant-woman-attacked/index.html.

2. Brad Scott, "Womb," Wildbranch Ministry, accessed November 15, 2017, https://www.wildbranch.org/teachings/word-studies/32womb.html.

3. Erin Kast, "Mercy of the Womb," *Peripateo* (Spring 2014), http://augustine collective.org/mercy-of-the-womb/.

4. David Cayley, *The Rivers North of the Future: The Testament of Ivan Illich* (Toronto: House of Anansi Press, 2005), 184.

5. Kast, "Mercy of the Womb."

6. Justin Taylor, "Ray Comfort's '180' Film on Hitler and Abortion," Gospel Coalition, September 30, 2011, https://www.thegospelcoalition.org/blogs/justin-taylor/ray-comforts-180-film-on-abortion/.

7. Matt Williams, "The Prodigal Son's Father Shouldn't Have Run!" *Biola Magazine* (Summer 2010), http://magazine.biola.edu/article/10-summer/the-prod igal-sons-father-shouldnt-have-run/.

8. François Fénelon, *Meditations on the Heart of God* (Orleans, MA: Paraclete Press, 1997), 161.

9. Dhananjay Mahapatral, "Over Twelve Thousand Farmer Suicides per Year, Centre Tells Supreme Court," *Times of India*, May 3, 2017, http://timesofindia .indiatimes.com/india/over-12000-farmer-suicides-per-year-centre-tells-supreme -court/articleshow/58486441.cms.

10. Raghavendra Madhu, "Tamil Nadu Farmer Protest: Forced to Choose Death over Disgrace," *The Quint*, April 24, 2017, https://www.thequint.com /blogs/2017/04/28/reasons-of-farmer-suicide.

11. "What Bodily Changes Can You Expect during Pregnancy?" Healthline, accessed November 15, 2017, http://www.healthline.com/health/pregnancy/bod ily-changes-during#HormonalChanges1.

12. Susan Scutti, "Pregnancy Changes a Mother's Brain for Years, Study Shows," CNN, April 26, 2017, http://www.cnn.com/2016/12/22/health/pregnan cy-brain-changes/.

13. Jeanne Segal, PhD, and Lawrence Robinson, "Volunteering and Its Surprising Benefits," Helpguide.org, accessed November 15, 2017, https://www.help guide.org/articles/healthy-living/volunteering-and-its-surprising-benefits.htm.

14. Sherrie Bourg Carter, "Helper's High: The Benefits (and Risks) of Altruism," *Psychology Today*, September 4, 2014, https://www.psychologytoday.com /blog/high-octane-women/201409/helpers-high-the-benefits-and-risks-altruism.

15. Segal and Robinson, "Volunteering."

16. Christine Carter, PhD, "What We Get When We Give," *Psychology Today*, February 19, 2010, https://www.psychologytoday.com/blog/raising-happiness/20 1002/what-we-get-when-we-give.

17. Carter, "What We Get."

18. "Fourteen Freed from Slavery in Indian Rock Quarry," IJM, September 30, 2008, https://www.ijm.org/news/14-freed-slavery-indian-rock-quarry.

Chapter 4 The Last Hour

1. "The Man in the Red Bandana," ESPN, video, accessed November 16, 2017, http://www.espn.com/video/clip?id=11505494.

2. "The Man in the Red Bandanna," CNN, accessed November 16, 2017, http://edition.cnn.com/SPECIALS/2002/america.remembers/stories/heroes/welles.html.

3. "Man in the Red Bandana," ESPN.

4. Kathleen Hennessey, "At 9/11 Memorial, President Obama Praises the Day's Heroes," *Los Angeles Times*, May 15, 2014, http://www.latimes.com/nation/nation now/la-na-nn-sept-11-memorial-president-obama-20140515-story.html.

5. Tom Rinaldi, *The Red Bandanna: A Life, a Choice, a Legacy* (New York: Penguin, 2016).

6. "Man in the Red Bandana, ESPN."

Chapter 5 A Price Paid

1. Keller, *Ministries of Mercy*, 100.

2. Keller, 100.

3. John MacArthur, *The MacArthur New Testament Commentary: Matthew 1–7* (Chicago: Moody, 1985), 192.

4. MacArthur, *MacArthur New Testament Commentary*, 195.

5. MacArthur, 195.

6. "The Federalist Papers: No. 74," Yale Law School, accessed November 20, 2017, http://avalon.law.yale.edu/18th_century/fed74.asp.

7. George Washington Digital Encyclopedia, s.v. "Whiskey Rebellion," accessed November 20, 2017, http://www.mountvernon.org/digital-encyclopedia /article/whiskey-rebellion/.

8. Mark Hughes, "The Number of Pardons Granted by U.S. Presidents Since 1789," Info Please, accessed November 20, 2017, https://www.infoplease.com /history-and-government/us-presidents/presidential-pardons.

9. Hughes, "Number of Pardons."

10. Ethan Trex, "Eleven Notable Presidential Pardons," CNN, January 5, 2009, http://www.cnn.com/2009/LIVING/wayoflife/01/05/mf.presidential.pardons /index.html?eref=rss_us.

11. "Mr. Lincoln's Office: Pardons and Clemency," Mr. Lincoln's White House, accessed November 20, 2017, http://www.mrlincolnswhitehouse.org/the-white -house/upstairs-at-the-white-house/upstairs-white-house-mr-lincolns-office/mr -lincolns-office-pardons-clemency/.

12. "The Innocence List," Death Penalty Information Center, accessed November 20, 2017, https://deathpenaltyinfo.org/innocence-list-those-freed-death-row.

13. "Executed but Possibly Innocent," Death Penalty Information Center, accessed November 20, 2017, https://deathpenaltyinfo.org/executed-possibly-innocent.

14. Laura Jarrett and Gloria Borger, "Obama Commutes Sentence of Chelsea Manning," CNN, January 18, 2017, http://www.cnn.com/2017/01/17/politics /chelsea-manning-sentence-commuted/.

15. Steven Nelson, "Obama Withholds Clemency from 'Pot Lifers,' Devastating Families," *U.S. News*, January 19, 2017, https://www.usnews.com/news/articles /2017-01-19/obama-withholds-clemency-from-pot-lifers-devastating-families.

16. Nelson, "Obama Withholds Clemency."

17. Jodi Wilgoren, "Four Death Row Inmates Are Pardoned," *New York Times*, January 11, 2003, http://www.nytimes.com/2003/01/11/us/4-death-row-inmates -are-pardoned.html.

18. Associated Press, "Illinois Governor's Blanket Pardon Spares Lives of 167 Condemned Inmates," Fox News, January 11, 2003, http://www.foxnews.com /story/2003/01/11/illinois-governor-blanket-pardon-spares-lives-167-condemned -inmates.html.

19. Associated Press, "Illinois Governor's Blanket Pardon."

20. Jens Manuel Krogstad, Jeffrey S. Passel, and D'Vera Cohn, "Five Facts about Illegal Immigration in the U.S.," Pew Research Center, April 27, 2017, http://www.pewresearch.org/fact-tank/2017/04/27/5-facts-about-illegal-immi gration-in-the-u-s/.

Chapter 6 In the Game

1. Gabriel Domínguez, "Modern-Day Slavery Widespread in India," Deutsche Welle, October 25, 2013, http://www.dw.com/en/modern-day-slavery-widespread -in-india/a-17180433.

2. Henri J. Nouwen, Donald P. McNeill, and Douglas A. Morrison, "Voluntary Displacement," *C21 Resources* (Fall 2014): 28–9, http://newspapers.bc.edu/cgi -bin/bostonsh?a=d&d=bcctor20140901-01.2.21.

3. Paulo Coelho (@paulocoelho), "There is only one thing that makes a dream impossible to achieve: the fear of failure," Twitter, February 7, 2014, https://twit ter.com/paulocoelho/status/431948014391799808?lang=en.

4. Keller, *Ministries of Mercy*, 13.

5. "How Many Nonprofit Organizations Are There in the U.S.?" Grantspace, accessed November 21, 2017, http://grantspace.org/tools/knowledge-base/Funding -Research/Statistics/number-of-nonprofits-in-the-u.s.

6. "Economic Impact," National Council of Nonprofits, accessed November 21, 2017, https://www.councilofnonprofits.org/economic-impact.

7. "Giving USA 2017: Total Charitable Donations Rise to New High of $390.05 Billion," Giving USA, June 12, 2017, https://givingusa.org/tag/charitable-giving/.

8. Peter Buffett, "The Charitable-Industrial Complex," *New York Times*, July 26, 2013, http://www.nytimes.com/2013/07/27/opinion/the-charitable-industrial -complex.html?_r=0.

9. Buffett, "Charitable-Industrial Complex."

10. Tess Srebro, "The U.S. Volunteer Rate Is Still Dropping. Why?" *Engaging Volunteers* (blog), March 25, 2016, http://blogs.volunteermatch.org/engaging volunteers/2016/03/25/the-u-s-volunteer-rate-is-still-dropping-why/.

11. Srebro, "Volunteer Rate."

12. Wikipedia, s.v. "Jewish Views on Love," last modified on October 30, 2017, 13:07, https://en.wikipedia.org/wiki/Jewish_views_on_love.

13. Tracy Jan, "Here's How Much You Would Need to Afford Rent in Your State," *Washington Post*, June 8, 2017, https://www.washingtonpost.com/news/wonk/wp/2017/06/08/heres-how-much-you-would-need-to-make-to-afford-housing-in-your-state/?utm_term=.41301d34511f.

14. Ryan Stewart, "9 Bonhoeffer Quotes to Remember a Pastor who Resisted Evil Unto Death," *Sojourners*, April 8, 2016, https://sojo.net/articles/11-bon hoeffer-quotes-remember-pastor-who-resisted-evil-unto-death.

Chapter 7 Hallelujah

1. Alex Tizon, "My Family's Slave," *The Atlantic* (June 2017), https://www.theatlantic.com/magazine/archive/2017/06/lolas-story/524490/.

2. Alexander Pope, *An Essay on Criticism* (Mineola, NY: Dover, 1994), 17.

3. Pope Francis, *The Name of God Is Mercy*, 26.

4. Edward Behr, *The Complete Book of Les Misérables* (New York: Arcade, 2016), 166.

5. Behr, *Complete Book*, 166.

6. Eve Fairbanks, "I Have Sinned against the Lord and against You! Will You Forgive Me?" *New Republic*, June 18, 2014, https://newrepublic.com/article/118 135/adriaan-vlok-ex-apartheid-leader-washes-feet-and-seeks-redemption.

7. Reimagine Stewardship Small Group Study, "Lesson 6: Stewarding Your Relationships—Teaching Segment with Shaunti Feldhahn," The Reimagine Group, video, 1:30.

8. Fairbanks, "I Have Sinned."

9. Sibusiso Tshabalala, "Washing Past Victims' Feet Won't Redeem This Former Apartheid Leader," Quartz Africa, October 7, 2015, https://qz.com/517401/wash ing-past-victims-feet-wont-redeem-this-former-apartheid-leader/.

10. Fairbanks, "I Have Sinned."

11. Ben Sheppard, "Apartheid Minister Vlok Seeks Redemption in Township Work," *Mail & Guardian*, October 5, 2015, https://mg.co.za/article/2015-10-05-ds.

12. Fairbanks, "I Have Sinned."

13. Claude Alexander, "Understanding Racism," Venture Christian Church, May 1, 2017, video, 11:30, http://venture.cc/sermons/2017/5/1/understanding-rac ism?rq=Bishop%20Claude%20Alexander.

14. Martin Magnusson, "No Rights Which the White Man Was Bound to Respect," American Constitution Society for Law and Policy, March 19, 2007, https://www.acslaw.org/acsblog/no-rights-which-the-white-man-was-bound-to-respect.

15. Claude Alexander, "Understanding Racism," video, 16:52.

16. NAACP, "History of Lynching," accessed December 14, 2017, http://www.naacp.org/history-of-lynchings/.

17. Claude Alexander, "Understanding Racism," video, 23:02–23:20.

18. "Love the Sinner," *The Economist*, October 22, 2015, http://www.econo mist.com/news/united-states/21676796-bittersweet-tale-prejudice-overcome-and -enduring-deep-south-love-sinner.

19. "Southern Baptists Apologize for Slavery Stance," NPR, August 28, 2009, http://www.npr.org/templates/story/story.php?storyId=112329862.

20. Martin Luther King Jr., "Letter from a Birmingham Jail [King, Jr.]," University of Pennsylvania—African Studies Center, April 16, 1963, https://www .africa.upenn.edu/Articles_Gen/Letter_Birmingham.html.

21. "Pete and Deb Ochs—Jailhouse Generosity," Vimeo, March 11, 2013, video, 7:28, https://vimeo.com/61562068.

22. "Christian Band MercyMe Opens Up about Abuse, God, and New Album," Fox News, April 22, 2014, http://www.foxnews.com/entertainment/2014/04/22 /christian-band-mercyme-opens-up-about-grace-god-and-new-album.html.

Chapter 8 The Two Deals

1. Alan Richardson, *A Theological Word Book of the Bible* (NY: MacMillan, 1951), 136–37.

2. Paul E. Miller, *A Loving Life: In a World of Broken Relationships* (Wheaton, IL: Crossway, 2014), 42.

3. Miller, *A Loving Life*, 42.

4. G. K. Chesterton, *What's Wrong with the World?* (CreateSpace, 2016), 26.

5. Wikipedia, s.v. "List of Baptist Denominations," last modified September 16, 2017, 12:32, https://en.wikipedia.org/wiki/List_of_Baptist_denominations.

Chapter 9 The Covenant of Intimacy

1. Walter Brueggemann in discussion with the author, January 12, 2017.

2. A.W. Tozer, "Why We Must Think Rightly about God," reprinted excerpt from *The Knowledge of the Holy*, accessed December 14, 2017, https://www.cru .org/us/en/train-and-grow/spiritual-growth/core-christian-beliefs/why-we-must -think-rightly-about-god.html.

3. Rick Warren, "Being an Agent of Mercy in the World" (sermon), May 15, 2016, Saddleback Church, https://saddleback.com/watch/media/being-an-agent-of -mercy-in-the-world.

4. Alexander MacLaren, *MacLaren's Commentary: Expositions of Holy Scrip- ture* (Harrington, DE: Delmarva Publications, 2014), Kindle edition.

5. "Ephesians 2:4," *John Gill's Exposition of the Bible*, accessed November 27, 2017, http://www.biblestudytools.com/commentaries/gills-exposition-of-the -bible/ephesians-2-4.html.

6. "About," Giving Pledge, accessed November 27, 2017, https://givingpledge .org/About.aspx.

7. "About."

8. "Does Saltwater Make Wounds Heal Faster?" Wound Care Society, July 4, 2016, http://woundcaresociety.org/salt-water-make-wounds-heal-faster.

9. "Salt and the Function of Our Cells," Salt Association, accessed November 27, 2017, http://www.saltassociation.co.uk/education/salt-health/salt-function-cells/.

10. "Thirteen Impressive Benefits of Salt," Organic Facts, accessed November 27, 2017, https://www.organicfacts.net/health-benefits/other/health-benefits-of-salt.html.

11. "Impressive Benefits."

12. "Impressive Benefits."

13. "What Comes First: Thunder or Lightning?" Reference.com, accessed November 27, 2017, https://www.reference.com/science/comes-first-thunder-lightning-731d9a095b518251.

14. "Thunder or Lightning?"

15. Joseph Benson, *The New Testament of our Lord and Savior Jesus Christ* 1856, accessed, December 14, 2017, http://biblehub.com/commentaries/benson/ephesians/2.htm.

16. Dietrich Bonhoeffer, *The Cost of Discipleship* (New York: Touchstone, 1959), 43.

Jack Alexander is chairman of The Reimagine Group and a senior fellow at the Sagamore Institute, heading up the generosity, mercy, and justice initiative, and has rich experience leading a variety of businesses. A previous recipient of an Ernst & Young National Entrepreneur of the Year Award, he is a regular speaker, coach, and advisor. He and his wife, Lisa, live in Atlanta. They have three grown sons and five grandchildren.

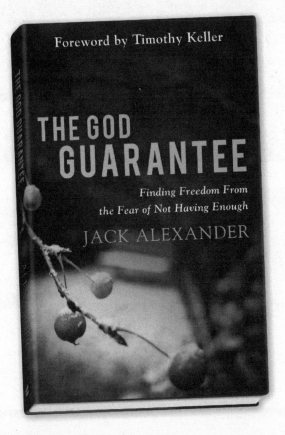

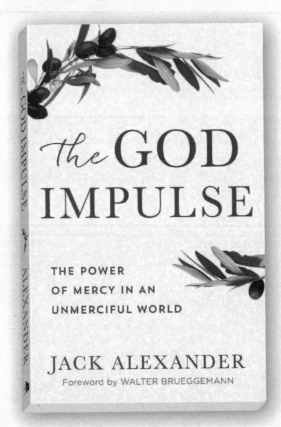